SMART
ORGANIZING

Simple Strategies for Bringing
Order to Your Home

Sandra Felton

The Organizer Lady™

Revell
Grand Rapids, Michigan

Published by Fleming H. Revell
a division of Baker Publishing Group
P.O. Box 6287, Grand Rapids, MI 49516-6287

Fifth printing, January 2006

Printed in the United States of America

Library of Congress Cataloging-in-Publication Data
Felton, Sandra.
   Smart organizing : simple strategies for bringing order to your home / Sandra Felton.
       p.   cm.
   Includes bibliographical references.
   ISBN 10: 0-8007-5978-8 (pbk.)
   ISBN 978-0-8007-5978-0 (pbk.)
   1. House cleaning. 2. Time management. I. Title
TX324.F4435 2005
648'.5—dc22   2004018541

The Organizer Lady and Bare Bones Way are trademarks of Messies Anonymous.

Scripture is taken from the HOLY BIBLE, NEW INTERNATIONAL VERSION®. NIV®. Copyright © 1973, 1978, 1984 by International Bible Society. Used by permmission of Zondervan. All rights reserved.

Contents

Thanks

I owe a lot to many people for helping me make this book what it is.

I appreciate the confidence my publisher, Fleming H. Revell, has placed in me over the past twenty years and continues to place in me as evidenced by this book. Bill Petersen and I have worked together over many of those twenty years. Special appreciation to the other editors who work so professionally to make it all come out right.

I want to say thanks to my critique group, headed by Karen Whiting, for their valuable input and suggestions. They don't let me get by with much, but I did think it was a little rude when they laughed at my dramatic flair passage—which has since been deleted.

Special thanks to the sixteen professional organizers who shared their outlooks in contributions on various topics throughout the book. Thanks to many others who made excellent contributions, which I could not fit into the book but were appreciated nonetheless.

The hardworking women in the trenches add a strong dose of realism and a lot of great information because they are right at the spots where the battle rages.

Thanks to my agent, Bruce Barbour, who has come on board and made a significant difference, and to my daughter-in-law, Linda Felton, for her perceptive final reading.

And as always, a big kiss and hug to my husband, Ivan, for doing extra work around the house so I could write. Otherwise my book would have gone forward while the condition of the house went backward. Find your own personal "Ivan" is my first tip.

Can We Talk?
Here's My Guarantee

Life is like a wild horse that wants to roam all over the track and, if possible, jump the rail and run amok without direction. Life veers toward complexity. Left to itself, your life will become more and more complicated, cluttered, and busy.

Life complicates itself naturally without assistance. That's the reason there are books called "Simplify Your Life" but none called "Complicate Your Life." A complicated life is stressful and unpleasant; a simplified life is peaceful and fulfilling.

We learned in physics class the second law of thermodynamics, which indicates in a general way that everything moves naturally toward chaos. So we spend a lot of time in our lives trying to address the problem of chaos, using handheld organizers like Palm Pilots, calendar systems, and books on organizing in an effort to stop the pell-mell rush to randomness in our lives.

We yearn for order. Our minds, our hearts, our souls thirst for simplicity and harmony, but they don't come as easily as we would like. The battle for order is hard won. Deep down we resist this fact. We hope that somehow nature will reverse its path toward complexity and we can become organized without much effort. For most of us, this is a pipe dream that will never come true.

However, as we look around, we notice that some people do seem to live naturally organized lives. By learning and following their simple "secrets," we can lead the kind of stress-free lives we crave. Don't get me wrong—nobody wants to live a boring life, stripped to its bare necessities. We all have our special desires, places in our lives we want to give the full treatment, maybe even go overboard from time to time. But what we want to avoid is letting life get so out of control that we don't have time to direct and focus it on the important things, because the unimportant things have taken up all the time.

Don't be more organized than you need to be, but don't be any less either. This book is about your reaching the organization goal you want in the simplest way possible. And then, if and when you have found the balance you want, you can move on to whatever extras you want to add. Simplicity is assured. Complexity is optional.

For more than twenty years, I have been known as the Organizer Lady. I entered the organizing field as a result of my own search for order in my chaotic life and in the process developed a keen sense of the internal and psychological working of organizing. In this book my insights will open mental and emotional doors that will enable you to bring your life to the level of orderliness you seek.

To help you in your search and make it more fun as well, the following chapters deal with the practicalities of organizing and often, but not always, contain the following:

- *Professional Organizer Viewpoints*. Over the last twenty years, professional organizing has taken its place with interior design and many other services that meet the needs of modern living. Professional organizers, many of whom are members of the National Association of Professional Organizers (NAPO, www .napo.org), the National Study Group on Chronic Disorganization (NSGCD, www.nsgcd.com), or both, share their expertise on various topics. While I can't vouch for each one specifically, I can tell you that if you find the right professional organizer at the right time, it can be a wonderful help for your organizational progress.

- *In the Trenches with Smart Homemakers.* People who are on the road to better organizing are enthusiastic about what they are doing. They love to share and hear from others who are on the same road. The comments of those in the trenches are the happy sharing of successes, techniques, or motivation that will encourage all of us.

  Being disorganized is a private matter for many people. Even so, some want to reach out to others for support. These postings are presented as they were written, casually, in email form, on forums on www.messies.com. The unique styles are not edited, so you will sense the personality of the writers. Their comments will not always dovetail with the suggestions given in the book, but they are valuable alternatives.

  Stories and anecdotes about people are based on real lives, but many names are altered.
- *Tips.* In this book I stick with tips that may be useful in getting the basics done. Any tip that makes your life easier and better is worthwhile. Any tip that doesn't meet your needs on a practical level in what you do daily should be totally ignored.

- *What Do You Want?* In almost every chapter you will find an evaluation to help you decide what level of housekeeping you are aiming for. Sometimes the evaluation will help you determine where you are so you can plan where to go from there.

  Remember, if you aim at nothing definite, you will likely hit it. That leads to discouragement. If you have a definite goal, you are much more likely to achieve it. Nothing can be more satisfying. Even if you don't fully achieve your highest goal, you will be farther down the road; and later, after you catch your breath, you can continue the journey.

- *The Bare Bones Way.* The Bare Bones Way is housekeeping cut to the bone. This section is focused on simple methods for getting the most out of life with the least effort. I call it the plump life, the quality of life you want for yourself and your family.

  I am giving you a heads-up here so you will be sure to note the most important part—the heart—of the book. There are ten simple steps or activities (Only ten steps! You can do that!) that if you do really get them and then *do* them, I guarantee you will maximize the fullness of living with minimum effort.

  Here are the ten activities that everyone can do:

- 3 *Steps* to organize the house so it works well—and easily.
- 2 *Routines* that maintain the house.
- 5 *Habits* to keep clutter on the run.

Now here's the guarantee: *Buy into these activities and integrate them into your life, and your housekeeping will be transformed "like magic."*

- *Beyond Bare Bones*. Sometimes we want to move above and beyond the basics. We may feel the urge to do something special in a single area, or our circumstances may regularly require more advanced techniques. Beyond Bare Bones suggests additional tips and ideas you may want to use.
- *Decision Time*. Nothing in the house or your life will change unless *you* do. Each of the chapters that deals with specifics of organization will guide you to decisions that will move you into order. Take them seriously. Perhaps you will want to keep a little notebook containing the decisions you make and evaluate them all when you get to the end of the book. Then you can choose the things you can do that will give you the most bang for your organizational-time-and-effort buck.

At the end of the book you will have a final look at your game plan for success. It is never overwhelming because we focus on only a few significant steps that will make a substantial difference.

One more word is in order. To make the book as helpful as possible, websites, phone numbers, and addresses are included. Over time, these may change, but a good search engine on the Internet will locate many of them and calling 800-555-1212 will help you find the phone numbers you need.

Part 1

Planning the Work

1

Improving Your Quality of Life

Values Nourish Your Soul

What do you value in life? What is important to you? You must establish what you value before you can prioritize your time and activities. Once that is done, focus on these things without fail in some way, large or small, every single day.

Since my four-year-old daughter, Caleigh, is my top priority, I make sure I focus on quality time with her. As a single parent and business owner, life can get pretty hectic. Each day I stop and focus completely on Caleigh and what she needs, whether it be for fifteen minutes or five hours. Prioritizing what I value most alleviates the stress-causing guilt I feel as a busy woman and mother.

Whether it be your children, your church, your volunteerism or your pet, to honor your values nourishes the soul and frees the mind to accomplish the goals that you set and the every-day tasks of life.

Charlotte Steill
Simply Put Organizing
Phoenix, Arizona
www.simplyputorganizing.net

When the Bough Breaks

- Nora knew her organizational cradle had fallen (so to speak) when she realized she was sorry her son's baseball team had gone into the finals. That forced her to extend her harried chauffeuring schedule that would now overlap with the schedule for a sport her other son was starting. *What kind of mother am I to resent my son's winning?* she asked herself. In the evening she also had to chauffeur her daughter who was involved in a community play. And the two boys were homeschooled to boot. Her husband tried to help, but he worked a job and a half. So Nora had to give up her hobby of going to garage sales, and the condition of her house became serious.

- The moment of truth came for the Parsons when they arrived an hour late to a get-together with a group of friends. Despite their best efforts, they just had not been able to juggle all the family activities, including supervising homework and eating a quickie dinner of frozen chicken nuggets—again. Rhonda was a stay-at-home mom who squeezed housework into the time when the kids were at school and when she wasn't participating in school, church, sports, and community events. She recognized the importance of these activities and didn't want to drop any of them. Her solution to the time crunch was to learn to dovetail the family's many activities more efficiently.

- On the other hand, her husband was exhausted by the frantic schedule he kept when he got home from his pressured job. He wanted to jettison many of their activities and spend more family time at home. They disagreed on how to solve the problem. She wanted to tighten the schedule; he wanted to simplify.

- Ruth and Ben are retired. They say what many retirees say: They don't know how they ever found time for jobs when they worked. Only by aggressively following a housekeeping schedule are they able to keep the clothes washed, the dishes done, and the house presentable (more or less). Both are experiencing health problems and, although they were active, now they don't have the energy they used to. The goal of neatness is becoming more elusive. They are thinking about downsizing so they will have less house and fewer belongings to maintain. But are they really up for making the change?

- Kara is a single mom with two teenage boys. Her older son, who has an interest in economics, quips that the family's chief import is pizza and their chief export is pizza boxes. None of the family members is particularly messy but they are all definitely casual about keeping a routine and setting goals for their lifestyle and the house. They sail close to the wind concerning organizational excellence. It doesn't take much for the house to slip into the deficit zone.

- Roger lives alone, works from home, and is deluged by paper. He is thinking of signing up for a Messiest Desk contest run by a local newspaper, so he can win a professional organizer makeover. He has little notes stashed all around. Tax info lies here and there with no particular order. He knows his carelessness

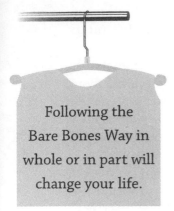

Following the Bare Bones Way in whole or in part will change your life.

will rise up to bite him someday soon. When his customers call, he is embarrassed when he can't quickly find information about their accounts. He has to stall and call them back later when, and if, he finds the missing information. Paperwork is his downfall. If the truth were known, the rest of the house is not very presentable either.

Behind the Bare Bones Story

Your story may differ from those above, but, if you are like most people today, you are asking yourself if there isn't a more agreeable way to live your life. You suspect you could do things better. You are probably right.

This book contains a specific approach to organizing. It is called the Bare Bones Way. Following the Bare Bones Way in whole or in part will change your life. Though the goal of the book is easier and more efficient organizing and cleaning, it goes well beyond that. The true goal is improved relationships, friendships, family, and self care. It is about quality of life. Ultimately it is about your fulfilling the purpose for which God put you on the earth.

Your house is not just a functional building with utilitarian furniture and personal belongings. In the book *Mrs. Dunwoody's Excellent Instructions for Homekeeping*, Mrs. Dunwoody, also known as Big Mama more for her presence than her size, is a slightly aristocratic Southern lady of yesteryear who brought a perspective to "homekeeping" that is often overlooked today. "She . . . believed that the ordinary acts we practice everyday at home are of more importance than their simplicity might suggest."[1] In one place Mrs. Dunwoody wrote, "Home is a sacred place for you and your family. Home interprets heaven."[2] In another she wrote about the home, "Others will suffer if you do not tend to it properly."[3]

Home interprets heaven.

Big Mama is right on. Consistently coming home to a well-cared-for environment makes everyone feel nurtured and secure. Comfort and a deep-down feeling of safety enable everyone who lives in a well-run household to live life to its fullest. No building can do that. But a home can.

A well-organized house and life are the foundation of a life well lived.

Organize to Sing Your Song

The reason we organize is so we will have fulfillment in our lives. If you insist on living life to its fullest, not dying with your song unsung or poorly sung, your life will have to be organized. There is no way around it because a well-organized house and life are the foundation of a life well lived.

Your heart has got to be in it. Organizing better because that is the right thing to do (your husband or mother or mother-in-law demands improvement) is an external motivation. You can do it that way, but the whole thing will be a drag. If you focus on a goal that means something personal to you, such as walking after work into a supportive and harmonious home, getting the children off to school without hassle, having happy family meals, easily giving a party, and in general being your best self, organizing will make sense. Internal focus will inexorably move the various aspects of your life, including the house, into place. Somewhat happily, I might add.

If you develop and follow a schedule just to survive, to get out of the house on time in the morning, you will dutifully put one foot in front of the other. But if you think of your schedule as personal care or family care, you will follow it with a different attitude.

If you file papers because you have to get them out of the way, you will hate filing. But if you think of it as gaining comfortable control of a complex modern life so you won't be scared by unexpected and unpleasant news, it takes on a different cast.

Organizing is only the means to an end. That end is a better and easier life for you and those you love. You may call it a fulfilled life, a balanced life, a meaningful life. I call it a plumper and fuller life—the Bare Bones Way.

T. S. Eliot said it well: "Home is where one starts from. Our house is our home base, the springboard from which we launch into the world. The kind of home base which we have will determine the strength of our entry."

There Has to Be More to Life Than . . .

Many women are walking around in a fog of fatigue. They are straining to rise to some nameless challenge called "successful woman" or "wonderful mother." Goaded by the pattern they saw or imagined in their own moms, they strive to reach an exalted level. They stay up too late and work too hard to meet what they perceive to be society's standards. If they are mothers, especially of young children, and if they work outside the home as well, they feel like they are "drowning."

If you see yourself in this picture, come up for air just long enough to think about alternatives you may want to incorporate in your life, so you can slowly but surely rise from the overwork you have built into your day-to-day existence. Exchange your sleeplessness for comfort. Instead of fatigue, create a life over which you have established control.

Life will be easier and more satisfying in the end when you have control of it. Getting to that point is not necessarily easy, because it calls for the hardest of all pursuits—change. Change of attitudes, habits, thought patterns, and sometimes even how you relate to others in your home will be needed. Change calls for decision making and, to quote Hamlet, "there's the rub." You will have to:

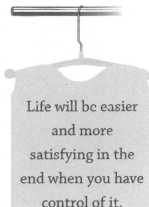

Life will be easier and more satisfying in the end when you have control of it.

- make decisions about your goals
- decide what system is the shortest route to reach your goals

We will have success, not because we are dealt a good hand but because we play well whatever we're dealt. Here is the key to playing well whatever hand you have been dealt. An Italian economist named Prieto discovered the 80/20 principle now accepted and applied in many different areas. He found that 80 percent of the wealth of Italy was in the hands of 20 percent of the population. Since that time, people have noticed that this same ratio applies broadly. School principals noticed that 20 percent of the students required 80 percent of the attention for discipline. Businesses noticed that 20 percent of the salespeople made 80 percent of the sales. While it does not always split down the 80/20 line exactly, nonetheless the principle is often evident. It is clear there is a small but significant factor that is really important in whatever we do. If we concentrate on that part (the 20 percent), most of our work will be cared for (the 80 percent).

This is an intriguing concept to apply in our homes. If we can isolate those most important factors that make housework go easily and well, we have a powerful tool, the secret of living a plumper and more fulfilling life with less effort.

Identifying the 20 Percent

Organizing can be a seductively problematic thing. Women can carry organizing to such an extreme that lives are built around keeping up the level of organizing already set up. Obviously, this is not the best approach.

No one needs to be 100 percent organized or even 80 percent organized. Just find the significant 20 percent that will accomplish what you want and do it. Prieto's principle keeps us from drifting into doing too much, keeping too much, being interested in too much, and generally overextending ourselves into a stressful situation.

More is not necessarily better. Often it is worse. As quantities increase, what started out as good and helpful evolves into a negative. Simple examples of this are all around us. Warm water in a shower is wonderful, but very hot water scalds. Helpful medication can cause death if taken in very high doses. One piece of Key Lime pie is delicious but eating a whole pie is sickening. Our tendency to overdo is often where we should look for the source of our organization problem. A certain amount (the important 20 percent) is good, helpful, and pleasant. The urge to do 100 percent boomerangs and becomes a negative.

Keeping too many mementos, pets (cats often), papers, and clothes balloons into a problem. This also happens with activities. Trying to accomplish more than any one person can without asking for help, volunteering excessively, and working long hours are characteristic of people who fail to prioritize and focus on the top 20 percent.

One woman who was expecting her mother for a weeklong visit concentrated on cleaning the oven even though the rest of the house needed attention. Obviously, the oven was not a part of the important 20 percent. She should have picked three major activities that would have made a significant impact.

For some women, keeping an excellently organized and sparkling clean house seems to be essential to happiness. Ann states that she feels better "at a cellular level" when the kitchen is immaculate and her tennis shoes are gleaming white. Rita goes home from work each day at lunch to handle the mail that was put in the mailbox in the morning, because she wants no task left undone for even a short time. Some super-organized people tie ribbons around their neatly folded sheet sets and pay special attention to how carefully the dog's blanket is folded.

This high organizational level is not healthy and interferes with maintaining relationships. The focus is all wrong and it misuses time. Those who seem to require this kind of control need to address the problem of trying to be 100 percent organized, which has unbalanced their lives, and they should search for the important 20 percent instead.

People who struggle with organizing often fail to understand Pricto's principle. They think more of a good thing makes everything better. Often this is not the case. The saying "Less is more" comes into play here. Bare Bones organizing keeps misplaced excesses from unexpectedly overtaking us. When we limit ourselves to doing just a few important things well, we are much more encouraged to think we can accomplish what we set out to do and be willing to give it a try. Anything you can do to get on the right track and stay there is well worth incorporating into your life.

When I Grow Up, I Want to Have . . .

Sometimes we get so caught up in the day-to-day workings of life, we forget what is really important. Looking back at what we longed for when we were younger will help us to remember. When you were a little girl (or boy) and thought of growing up, what kind of house did you dream of living in? Was it a house that looked like yours does now?

Imagine that you are that little elementary-school-age child somehow transported into your future and walking into your house today. Would you be happy and pleased that it is yours? What part would delight you? What part would you want to change?

It is not too late to create the home you yearned for back then. Don't settle for less than what you really want. Don't trade off your dreams for things that don't satisfy. You can do that without realizing what you are doing.

Home is so much more than a place to eat, sleep, bathe, and change clothes. It is where we express ourselves to others and to ourselves. It is a friend we create to comfort ourselves.

When you look around your home, do you see yourself mirrored there or do you live in the house of a stranger? Do you honor your childhood dreams?

In this context, Bare Bones organizing is gathering up those scattered and forgotten dreams and making them come true in the surest and least complicated way.

What Do You Really Want? Remembering Your Dreams

Here is a little quiz for you. Choose a response to complete each of the statements below.

If there were no obstacles of time, money, or energy, what would you want?

1. I want my house to look like:
   a. a gorgeous house as in the magazines
   b. a beautiful house like the house of my friend who is good at decorating
   c. a nice house like the house of my friend who seems to keep things up well
   d. a comfortable house that looks good enough for family and close friends
   c. other (explain)

2. The areas I am most interested in improving are:
   a. every room
   b. most rooms in the central core of the house, excluding the basement, attic, storerooms, and maybe the kids' rooms
   c. the public rooms only (those seen by visitors, plus the bathroom)
   d. the living room
   e. the storage areas, like the basement, garage, attic, and the like

3. The level of organizing I am aiming for is:
   a. beautiful and impressive
   b. presentable to company
   c. neat looking in general
   d. orderly and working well

4. The frequency I want this is:
   a. always
   b. usually
   c. on the weekends or other specific occasions
   d. when guests come

5. My motivation for wanting to improve is (choose all that apply):
   a. for me to enjoy
   b. for my family to enjoy
   c. for guests
   d. to teach my children how to live
   e. to make my spouse and other important people happy

6. My level of emotion concerning my approach to my house:
   a. I yearn desperately for change.
   b. I strongly desire change.
   c. I really want change.
   d. I would like change.

Decision Time—Choose Your Top 20 Percent

Now write these six sentences into a short paragraph making use of the words and ideas above or using your own words.

I want my house to look like (see 1 above)_____
_____. I want to improve (2 above) _____
_____. I hope it will turn
out to be (3 above)_____
(how often—4 above) _____. The
reason I want to make these changes is/are (5 above)_____
_____. I _____
_____ (from 6 above).

2

Get a Simple Plan and Simply Work the Plan

Settling into Order

It took me a long time to discover that I was trying to live successfully with no priorities. I find many other people have the same difficulty.

As one who started life rather disorganized, I want to hold out encouragement to anyone who wants to improve. I watched myself, and now others, begin and move through this transforming process. The thing is, it is not just about lining things up in tidy stacks. It is a whole turning toward another way of viewing life. It is about seeing that there is a subtle order throughout nature that is pervasive, that there is actually a natural balance to things. That as we look for, or open ourselves toward, the element of balance, of symmetry, of moderation in everything, we slowly begin to settle into order. The main thing is to eliminate the excess; whether possessions,

25

> It comes down to great execution of the basics, day after day, year after year. That's what leads to greatness.

activities, mental busyness, or overwork. Then order can return. It is actually the path of least resistance.

Frances Strassman
More Than Order
Berkeley, California
www.morethanorder.com

Is There a Silver Bullet?

When Burger King Corporation found itself in trouble, the management decided they needed to reorganize. They hired both a new CEO and a new president to try to raise their slumping sales. We can learn from what these two business gurus have to say about how to improve.

When talking about their plans for turning the business around, the CEO Brad Blum said, "We are not looking for a quick hit. There are no silver bullets here." He went on to say Burger King is going to stick to basic goals. For them that means focusing on three things: making sure the restaurants are clean; serving hot, good-tasting food; and filling orders quickly and accurately. Their goals are focused and clear.

The new president, Bob Nilsen, agreed that sustained focus on basics is what gets the job done. "It comes down to great execution of the basics, day after day, year after year," he said. "That's what leads to greatness."[1]

IN THE TRENCHES WITH SMART HOMEMAKERS

Life is a Rubik cube; you can't choose or move one thing without moving everything else. You have to take a look at the cube and find the level of cleanliness that puts the most pieces into place. Depending on where your life is, that can vary.

Take-Charge Action Attitudes

There are certain decisions and choices you must make as you determine a plan and set it in motion.

- Decide what you really want. Is something hurting you, your family, or your friends? Could it be better?
- Choose your level. Good enough is good enough; what does that mean to you?
- Challenge old thinking. Welcome flexibility and change.
- Keep your focus. Narrow your goals and choose your activities to meet your goals.
- KISS—Keep It Super Simple. Avoid unnecessary complexity.
- Look farther ahead. Develop a clear vision for what you want.
- Ease into order. Start small and keep adding steps to further your progress.
- Factor in "outside help." Be willing, even anxious, to reach out to others for assistance.
- Eliminate the small stuff in your plans. Concentrate only on the things that will make a significant difference.
- Once you identify the few big things, attend to them in detail. Make sure you succeed in the activities you designate as important.

The Bare Bones Way

Basics of the House

Gurus from every discipline say the same thing, whether it is a business like Burger King, sports, cook-

27

ing, or, in our case, organizing the house. Success follows the people who narrow down the few important goals they want to accomplish and pursue those few things with vigor.

First, narrow your goals. What are the most important things you want? Or suppose you had ten distinct wishes for your house (and no more), what would those wishes be? List below the ten things you would change if there were no limitations of space, time, money, or energy. Later, you will have the opportunity to put these ideas together in a motivating overview of your goals.

If I had ten wishes for my house, I would wish:

1.
2.
3.
4.
5.
6.
7.
8.
9.
10.

Then, in a separate list, which you will post somewhere for frequent reference, isolate and concentrate on the three most important wishes. Later choose three more for emphasis until they all, or the most significant, are accomplished.

1.
2.
3.

Hardwired for Order

As we consider going forward, we need to stop to ask ourselves how much we really want to upgrade the condition of our house. Is it worth the effort? Don't we work hard enough outside the home? Why not take a laid-back, relaxed approach? "I don't want to stay on my guard at home, working there as well as outside," we may say. "I don't want to be on the kids' backs in the little time we have together."

These are serious considerations, but our choice is not that simple. The condition of our home has implications that reach farther than may be obvious. Our surroundings are inextricably linked to our psyches. People who live in slums with trash, graffiti, and broken plumbing are at a distinct disadvantage for personal success. Their surroundings drag them down.

How does this relationship work? I knew that the police have begun to clean up and beautify neighborhoods because they have become aware of the connection between physical surroundings and crime, so that's where I went for answers.

"Why are surroundings so important?" I asked my friend, a career policeman who had been a detective in a major city, the police chief of a smaller one, and was now an instructor-coordinator at a police academy. He had dealt with cleaning up neighborhoods on a community level.

"When God created us," he said going to the spiritual roots of the problem, "he hardwired us to be in his image. Part of that is he put into our hearts a desire for order and beauty, since both are important to him." He went on to explain the discouragement of people who feel powerless to control their environment. Broken windows, derelict cars, uncollected garbage, litter, and graffiti overwhelm hope and trample pride. When the spirit of people is broken, criminal elements drift in unchallenged. In short,

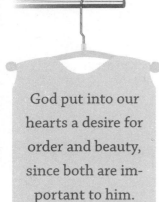

clutter eats away what is best in us as humans.

So it is with our houses. William James said, "Nothing is so fatiguing as the eternal hanging on of uncompleted tasks." Rationalizing can't change the fact that living in clutter discourages and fatigues us, whereas living in an orderly house builds pride of the right kind within us.

> God put into our hearts a desire for order and beauty, since both are important to him.

I'm not talking about perfectionism, where the house has got to look like a model home. I'm talking about walking into a place that supports and encourages us, that lures our family to come home for rest, that offers respite to our friends—in short, "home" at its best.

More Order/Less Work

If you are searching for a few tips to further upgrade an already elaborate system of organizing, this is not the book for you. On the other hand, if you want to move yourself (and your family or business) forward in life as effortlessly as possible, keep reading. As you apply what you read, you will desert breathless rushing about and seek instead a serene effectiveness in ordering your life.

Most of us do not go overboard, in keeping things neat. The majority of us have reasonable standards. In general, each of us wants the following:

- We want to be acceptably organized, to avoid breakdowns in organizing that cause emergencies in our jobs and our home lives.
- We want to spend less time on keeping our heads above water in the myriad of activities we have to do. We want to struggle less or not at all.

- We want to keep our focus on relationships, using our house and our time to make meaningful contributions to those we love and to our community. We want to live our lives significantly by investing in the important things, not just the urgent things.

Do less but achieve more. This is the Bare Bones motto.

Disorganization keeps us from these goals. Having to spend copious amounts of time and energy to get and stay organized hinders our success. So we seek a way to get maximally organized while putting out a minimum of effort. To put it another way, we want to do less but achieve more. This is the Bare Bones motto.

We Succeed with KISS

So how can we do this? The secret is simplicity. Old-fashioned mottos stick with us because they ring true in a practical way. The motto that applies here is KISS, which (contrary to what you may have heard previously) is an acronym for Keep It Super Simple. In this complex world, people who succeed easily do it because they get a simple plan and simply work the plan.

Complexity surrounds us. Cut out the unnecessary complications and get down to the essentials of organizing. Free yourself to move forward simply and successfully.

Ten Powerful Ideas

You will find that the heart of the book consists of ten powerful ideas that will transform your house and life. Grab these and hold on to them. The first three are steps that get the house under control; the last seven are ways to keep it that way. In the rest of this book, we will be looking at these steps, routines, and habits.

- 3 *Steps* to organize the house so it works well—and easily:
    Consolidate
    Containerize
    Condense
- 2 *Routines* that maintain the house:
    Four things in the morning
    Four things at night
- 5 *Habits* to keep clutter on the run:
    If you get it out, put it back.
    Apply the thirty-second rule consistently.
    Follow the camping rule today.
    Look, really look, at your surroundings.
    Use little minutes.

There will be many other organizing suggestions in this book. Ignore 80 percent of them for now. Choose to implement only those few (the significant 20 percent) that will impact your life right now.

Take Control

The choices you make and the plans you choose to implement flow from your inner self. If you allow your life to mold you instead of your taking control and molding your life, you will find only emptiness, uneasiness, depression, and inauthenticity. If you are willing to take control, you will discover your real self and will be able to live the life of the person you discover yourself to be. Finding a personal organizing system that works for you and developing yourself to the maximum are parts of that search for who you really are.

Housekeeping does not stand alone. It is hooked to a larger picture. Excellence in housekeeping affects our well-being because through it we recognize our power, strengths, and virtues. In other words, it is one of the playing fields on which we do important life business.

Whoa! you may say. All I want is not to have eight more hours of work when I get home from the office! I just want the kids to do their part. Something has got to be done about the menus. I want more time for rest and fun. Don't give me all this deep talk about character and discovering who I am.

> Excellence in housekeeping affects our well-being because through it we recognize our power, strengths, and virtues.

Okay, we'll move on to the hands-on stuff. But don't be surprised if you bump into something deeper as you challenge yourself to a better life. And don't be surprised if you delve into your heart as you move ahead in reaching your goal.

Decision Time—Choose Your Top 20 Percent

Take the three wishes you wrote out earlier and rewrite them as declarative statements of intent with a general time frame, such as:

I intend to organize the living room and set up a system to keep it that way by October 1.

I intend to train my family to work with me and have a schedule of their help in place by the end of the summer.

Organizing the House the Bare Bones Way

The Sacred Art of De-accumulation

De-accumulating can be a daunting task. It requires deci-sions. If we limit our decision-making energy by breaking down the task, we will be less likely to sabotage our project.

Begin by looking for the obvious "no decision-making energy required" items such as:

- trash
- things that belong elsewhere
- and things you know without thinking you do not need or care about—usually about 40 percent of what occupies our prime space

If you can't decide about an item in six seconds, move on to the next. This "I don't know pile" is usually about 20 percent of the task. Now do the math. You have reduced the items to actually organize to 40 percent, a manageable task.

Sue Marie Bowling
Prescription for Order
Brooke, Virginia
www.rx4order.com

Encouragement While Decluttering

Letting go is the first and biggest step in decluttering your life. Most people need the cool head of an interested but disengaged outsider to do it.

A lot of people try to do this with a sister, mother, or best friend. It may be that people whose lives are emotionally tied to yours aren't going to let you see your stuff with the clear eyes that the unsentimental journey of organizing your life requires. They'll say things that encourage you to keep your clutter without realizing it: "You're not going to get rid of that, are you? Didn't Mom give that to you? If you're not going to keep that, I want it."

Choose carefully a sympathetic but unentangled friend or hire outside help. You need someone who is not wrapped up with what you own or have in order to move forward without unnecessary roadblocks.

Cyndy Ratcliffe
Organizing Solutions, Inc.
Raleigh, North Carolina
www.organizingsolutions.biz

"Smart Lazy"

"If you are going to be lazy, be smart lazy. That's what my dad told me," said the waiter as he pulled out his neatly folded bills to give change. "So I stay organized. I always put my shoes in the same spot. I separate my money, the pennies from the other change. I keep my money from tips all in order while I work. That way I don't need to spend time looking for change. The other

I stay organized so I don't have to work so hard.

servers stick their money in any pocket. I tell them they are going to lose their tips," he said, hands flapping to show how the money would fly away. He continued telling how being organized works for him. "I stay organized so I don't have to work so hard. I don't let problems develop."

Unbeknownst to him, he was verbalizing the basic Bare Bones principle. Be lazy. That is, don't expend unnecessary energy. But be *smart* lazy. Set up your life for success. As we saw in the last chapter, this involves choosing a simple system that works for you and simply working that system—consistently.

You are not being asked to make big changes or take vows to live life totally differently from the way you are living now. That is unrealistic. You are being asked to make only a few consistent changes, the 20 percent that will make a significant impact on your organizational life. With less effort, you will upgrade your level of living.

Remember, the power to effect change can be found here:

- 3 *Steps* to organize the house so it works well—and easily.
- 2 *Routines* that maintain the house.
- 5 *Habits* to keep clutter on the run.

What Do You Want?

Evaluate yourself to determine your present style. Mark where you are on the lines.

1	2	3	4	5
High style is my way of life.			I like a *very* casual lifestyle.	

1	2	3	4	5
I am ready to streamline belongings.			I can't get rid of anything.	

1	2	3	4	5
I take storage very seriously.			I put things where it is convenient.	

1	2	3	4	5
I love to keep a regular routine.			I like a casual approach to routine.	

Look at the characteristics that you evaluated as close to 5. Begin with the one that is farthest to the right of the continuum, and challenge yourself to make changes in this area that will move you toward the left side. When you see progress, begin working on the others.

Steps of the Bare Bones Way

Change in any area of life occurs when the discomfort of remaining the same becomes greater than the discomfort of changing. Becoming organized is not complicated. It takes only three steps to bring order to your house.

Each step is equally important. There is no way to cut out any part of the three classic steps for organizing:

1. Consolidate
2. Containerize
3. Condense

These steps get the house under control. When these are followed by the two routines for maintenance, it will stay that way.

Consolidate

To consolidate means to bring things together or to join things into a whole. Look around your house. Your job, should you choose to accept it—and I sure hope you do—is to gather each and every one of your belongings into a group of similar things. For example, all of your gift-wrapping items, such as paper, ribbon, tape, and scissors (yes, scissors, even though you will need other pairs for other groupings) go together. Other groups are

- building tools and materials, such as screws and nails
- gardening tools and other gardening items
- craft supplies
- flower paraphernalia, such as vases and floral tape
- shoes for each individual
- hats and caps
- music items, such as CDs, tapes, electronic equipment
- cleaning products
- makeup
- important papers, bills
- books, magazines
- other groups that make sense to you in the way your house works

Put these groupings in temporary boxes or containers that you label with bold signs. Nice white banker's boxes, about 12 × 18 inches, bought in office supply stores, seem to work much better than used cartons you can pick up in grocery stores. Nice-looking white boxes signal your commitment to doing things the right way. When the tops are on the boxes, the things inside can't be seen, which eliminates the cluttered feel. If you use boxes from the grocery store, the house will look more junky while you are trying to create order. Put the boxes as near as possible to the place you think their contents belong. It may be on the shelf, in the proper cabinet, or close to the cabinet.

Doing this will bring reality into focus. Suddenly you notice that along with the regular tools you have five hammers of the same size and weight. Thirteen bottles of glue, a whole lot of snapshots, and many duplications of other things appear along with lost or forgotten items.

You will also realize that some things are junk that you will want to discard. Containerize these in a box or trash bag and get rid of them immediately. There will be things you are ambivalent about—you think you should discard but don't really want to; other things are good enough to give away. Put these in boxes that you label THINK ABOUT and GIVE AWAY.

While you are consolidating, the house tends to fall into temporary disarray, so break the job up into units you can handle during the available time periods. For example, isolate one closet, dejunk it, and organize it. Put the excess out of the way in boxes and, as soon as you are finished, discard what you don't want to keep. In this way you get the closet organized but the room still looks good.

Keep going with each project until you get it finished. If you have trouble finishing a project, ask for the assistance of supportive members of the family, invite a friend over to help, or hire someone to do the job for you.

Containerize

Once you see how many items you have of each grouping, you are ready to put the different groupings into

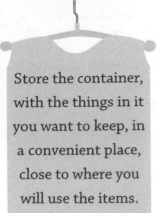

Store the container, with the things in it you want to keep, in a convenient place, close to where you will use the items.

containers, such as boxes, baskets, or whatever makes sense for what you have and where you have to place it.

When you see the size of your pile, evaluate the size of container you need, considering the space you have to store it. With tape measure in hand, find containers that meet your need. These may already be in the house, or you may have to buy some. Just be sure there is a container for each grouping.

When you see all that you have in each grouping, you may decide that you don't need it all, and you begin to decide to get rid of some of your stuff.

Store the container, with the things in it you want to keep, in a convenient place, close to where you will use the items. This is especially important if you use them often. Things used repeatedly should be put within easy reach. For example, office supplies should be in or near the desk; cleaning supplies in the bathroom and kitchen cupboards. Finally, label the front of the container (where possible) to indicate what is inside. If you have small children, include a picture as part of the label.

CHOOSING CONTAINERS

When deciding what containers are best for storing certain items, ask yourself two questions:

- Will items be easy to get out of this container when I need them?
- Will items be easy to return to this container?

If the item is hard to reach when you need to retrieve it, you will frustrate yourself. If what you have gotten out is difficult to return, you will be tempted to leave it out rather than struggle to put it back.

First Contain, Then Maintain

There are two important things to remember about containing your stuff. Do not crowd your items into a container, and do not crowd containers into storage space. It is hard to work with things that are jammed together. When you make your items easy to retrieve and return, your organizational life will benefit. First contain, then maintain.

If It Is Not Where It Belongs, It Might as Well Be Gone

Some people can get away with leaving things out of place or storing them poorly. It doesn't interfere with their routine or productivity. Many people—including me and maybe you too—can't. There are two reasons for this.

First, we don't seem to be able to locate things visually if they are out of place. Our eyes and mind go only to the one place we expected to find the item. If it is not there, we don't see it, even if it is a foot away from the designated spot. Our eyes just don't track in a way that will locate the item elsewhere. This is where the expression, "If it were a snake, it would have bitten you," comes from.

Almost everybody has had that experience at one time or another, but some of us have it as a way of life. For us, it is imperative to make sure things are consistently where they belong because if they are not there, they are pretty much gone. Do yourself a favor and take this part of storage seriously. Put everything in its place as you finish with it, so it will be there when you need it.

The second reason for consistently returning items to their specific places is because our memories falter early on in the search process. If an item is missing, some people can figure out an alternative place to look. They can guess, and pretty accurately for the most part, where else the item might be. By looking in three or four possible spots, they find it.

Not so for the rest of us. In his book on increasing output, Dr. Mel Levine alludes to his problem with keeping up with what he needs when he writes that he spends a lot of his day searching for misplaced objects. "If I need a Phillips screwdriver for a chore at home, it consumes much less time and anxiety if I buy a new one than if I try to locate the one I bought six weeks ago."[1] He also loses important papers at work. Obviously he would benefit from applying the three steps of organizing.

If the screwdriver is not in the place we expect to find it, many of us may look in one more spot and then give up and buy another one. If you do this often enough, the house becomes filled with many mislaid, duplicate glue bottles, rolls of tape, scissors, stamps, gift cards, flashlights, and a hundred other items that can be easily misplaced in the course of everyday life. Lost papers, some irreplaceable, hide in piles and other places, covering the desk and surfaces of the house.

Containerizing our things properly will save us money, time, and most of all, frustration.

Condense

No, "condense" doesn't mean to pack everything in tightly. Basically it means to get rid of excess belongings. You may wonder why this is the last step and not the first.

We declutter all along the way as we start to take control of the house. However, as a practical matter, it is when we see how much duplication we have, after we have sorted things into groups, that it really hits us, "I have w-a-a-y too much stuff!" At that point, we are able to let it go intelligently and with much more emotional clarity.

Though how much we should keep is a complex subject, it is safe to say that in today's world, we all keep "way too much stuff." The amount of things displayed from a single house at a garage or yard sale testifies further to the fact that many others are in the same boat we are.

Trying to live with all of these things is not easy. The more stuff we have, the more we have to manage. This kind of abundant life leads to many problems that have to do with our stuff:

- buying and paying for everything
- arranging things
- cleaning and dusting them
- storing them
- remembering where everything is
- learning how to use things
- disposing of unused stuff

IN THE TRENCHES WITH SMART HOMEMAKERS

We use things to try to fill the emptiness, tho hurts, the past and or present feelings of deprivation. We attach our longings, dreams, hopes, and desires to our stuff.

Special Cases

For one reason or another, some people feel the need to get and collect an unreasonable number of belongings. Even when they don't have room, energy, or ability to properly store the things they gather, they continue to fill the house until it becomes a jumbled warehouse. Serious problems ensue for these people. They hesitate to have repairmen or even firemen come into the house. Their families become concerned about the health and safety of their loved ones. Landlords are upset by the condition of the property. Sometimes neighbors call the civil authorities. Often nobody knows the condition of the house because the resident keeps outsiders away.

In these extreme cases, people may maintain homes full of belongings, or they may fill sheds or barns outside the house. Some rent storage units to hold all their stuff. The belongings may be clothes, gifts, furniture, books, or whatever appeals to them. The items may be bought at yard sales or new with tags still on them or still in the shopping bag.

When it gets to this extreme, the condition is called hoarding. Recently, the problem has been studied as a part of the psychological disorder known as obsessive-compulsive disorder. I mention it only because a few people reading this book for help may need to be aware of it, either for themselves or someone they care about, and should seek professional help. For the latest information on this problem, look up obsessive-compulsive disorder/hoarding on the Internet.

The Bare Bones method bogs down when too much stuff is in the picture. Fortunately, most of us are not dealing with a problem of this magnitude. Even so, it is common in today's world for many of us to try to keep more than is good for us. Excessive gathering boomerangs from promising to meet our needs to becoming a burden.

Tightly Controlled Clutter

Rose is an example of one who indulges in moderate excess. In her lovely home, she does not struggle

44

with neatness or with being unable to find things. Her belongings are well stored, and stored, and stored. She and her husband have a two-car garage into which one car can fit. The rest of the space is full of many items they use in their busy and interesting lives. These are on shelves or hung on the wall.

In the home office there is a bookcase full of books. There is also one in the family room. Her husband's office has walls of books. The bathroom has a large and tasteful basketful of magazines. There is a shed holding heavy tools in the backyard. Not a shred of clutter or crowding is evident. The house looks good, and both Rose and her husband can locate the items they need most of the time. They function well.

Like Rose, many people don't have a clutter or storage problem, but they do have two more subtle problems. One is management. They must work hard to manage all their belongings on a day-to-day basis. In addition, when the time comes to dismantle this household, it will be a very big job. However, this way of life works for these people because they handle it well.

Even so, if they were to reduce their belongings, perhaps by about 20 percent, they would probably experience an 80 percent improvement in the quality of their lives.

A Deliberate Choice

The wealth of our country makes it possible for us to overdo, even if we are not personally wealthy. Like fast-food outlets, we have supersized our lives in many ways. Simplicity is out; excess is in. We have grown so used to having too much that we have begun to believe it is normal and even necessary.

But change is in the air. There is a trend back to basics. The high-calorie-double-cheeseburger-with-bacon

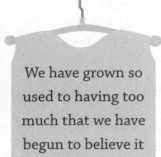

We have grown so used to having too much that we have begun to believe it is normal and even necessary.

sellers have begun to offer lighter fare. Realtors report that many who previously bought huge houses to make a big impression are returning to cozy, more personal homes. They want family members to talk face-to-face rather than cell phoning to the other end of the house or using the intercom.

In the past, the national economy forced the simple life on society at large. Now, with an improved economy, we must make a personal and deliberate choice to simplify, to draw back from materialism, and to seek a more harmonious way of life. It's a matter of quality replacing quantity, significance taking over for ostentation. This is not easy because it is so foreign to the familiar get-more mentality.

Sometimes simplicity is forced. Clara was removed from her home because it was deemed unsafe and unfit for her children due to hoarding and was placed in an apartment sparsely furnished by the Salvation Army. She had only a few of her personal belongings and reported that she felt great relief to be free of the burden of stuff. She vowed to continue to live free of excess.

When simplifying is voluntary, the Bare Bones Way can help.

IN THE TRENCHES WITH SMART HOMEMAKERS

From Janet:

Make for yourself a really small area to keep tidy. It may be some personal space (beside your bed) or it may be the bit that people see immediately when you open the door. Or it may be the place that really gets you annoyed. Just choose your own personal organized space—not too big—but well defined. (I recommend about 2–4 feet square—no bigger for the first bit.)

Then go through that space and you sort through everything that is there. You make 3 piles—stuff that really is JUNK—old receipts/junk mail/cardboard boxes/a single sock. My way of looking at it is "Have I needed this in the last 12 months? WILL I need it in the next 6 months?" If the answer is NO— throw this lot AWAY for good—no more to be seen. The second pile is "This is too much for me. I think I might need it, and I can't make up my mind." This goes in a box marked "sort later." The third pile is the giveaways—it is still good, but my neighbor may need it/use it etc.

Don't do all the sorting through at one time—the idea is not to run a marathon, but to teach you some new habits in getting the mess down.

Let Beauty Inspire You

Maintaining order is essential for a satisfactory life. How to maintain it will be detailed in chapter 6. But working for order is not nearly as emotionally satisfying as creating beauty. In the same way that it is more satisfying to save money than to pay off debts, it is more satisfying to create beauty than to dissipate clutter. For that reason we cannot ignore the need for a balance between the two.

I used to advise establishing order before trying to create beauty, but I learned that people need inspiration to motivate them to do the hard job of organizing. It is a delicate balance. We don't want to put cute trinkets in the midst of a mess and call it attractive decorating. On the other hand, we can use a focused pursuit of beauty to spur us on to a harmoniously organized life. We do it by creating areas or zones of beauty as we organize.

Some people choose a small area where they will maintain beauty, such as keeping the kitchen sink shiny

We can use a focused pursuit of beauty to spur us on to a harmoniously organized life.

or the kitchen counter clear and polished. Others start with one corner of the living room, keeping the lamp table polished as it sits beside the overstuffed chair with the comfy, attractive pillows. Perhaps some cut flowers grace the area. Relaxing in that spot of beauty and seeing it regularly in passing inspires and motivates these people to keep going.

Or we may aim at keeping an entire room beautiful. For instance, if we create a lovely bedroom, our desire for order will flow from it to the rest of the house. When we spend time in our sanctuary, we exit renewed and energized. The emotional satisfaction that is derived from what we have created will encourage us to continue spreading more and more order and beauty throughout the house.

More specific ideas on how to maintain the house will be given in chapter 6, but remember, the impetus to do it and do it consistently over the long term comes from a heart for beauty.

Tips

- Make sure you have a place where family members can easily store coats, book bags, and sports equipment as they enter the house. Hooks, cubbies, or shelves keep them from dropping things in the closest spot available. A bench on which they can sit while removing their shoes and boots is a good idea. If you are lucky, you may come across a bench that has drawers under the seat. The more double duty a piece of furniture is, the better, especially if it contains a storage unit.

- Make good use of organizational equipment and products. If you see something that solves a problem, seriously consider buying it, but avoid gadgets that will prove to be useless to you. I needed more towel hangers in the bathroom and got really excited when I saw a towel bar that hangs over a glass shower door—until I remembered that we don't have a glass shower door.

  Make sure the product will work in your setting. For example, if you have limited space, it may be a great idea to buy a step ladder/ironing board combo that folds flat for easy storage. A television supported by a vertical spring-tension pole eliminates the need for a piece of furniture to hold the TV. The pole fits between the floor and ceiling so the TV "floats" in the spot you place it. Though it may not be easy to find, the right product in the right situation can alleviate a lot of organizational problems.

- Donate to the nearest charity or the one that makes donating the easiest, such as Goodwill Industries, the Salvation Army, your local secondhand store, or any place that will pick up your donated items. If you have something that is stuck in your house because you can't find a place that will take it, try www.recycles.org for a list of nonprofits. Some charities interested in special items are:

  National Cristina Foundation (www.cristina.org)—old computers for use by the disabled

  Dress for Success (www.dressforsuccess.org)—good suits for people reentering the workforce

  Wireless Foundation (www.wirelessfoundation.org)—old cell phones to be used by victims of domestic violence (local collection sites can be found on the website)

  Lions Club (www.lionsclubs.org) or LensCrafters or other local eyeglass store—eyeglasses

Take note: Be charitable to yourself! If things like these have been lying around for weeks waiting to be sent to a "special" person or place, decide today to give them to a local charity or (gasp!) just discard them. The Bare Bones Way is just *do* it.

Decision Time

This chapter contains the heart—the three *C*s—of the Bare Bones Way for getting the house under control. Each step is necessary to set up the house for Bare Bones simplified living.

Consider how you will put these three action steps into practice. Focus on each one, then put a check beside each incremental step as you do it.

Consolidate

_____ Obtain boxes in which to gather groups of items.

_____ Group items into the boxes by category.

_____ Locate the box near the area where the items will be stored.

Containerize

_____ Note the size of the container you will need to store each group of items.

_____ Buy containers that will fit on the shelf and hold the things you are storing. You may want to measure before you go and take a tape measure to shop. It will take a while to collect the variety of baskets and containers you need.

_____ Place labels (with or without accompanying pictures) on the containers.

Condense

_____ Give away duplicates or unnecessary items.

_____ Throw away broken or useless items.

The Toilet Paper Test: Everybody buys it and uses it, but how individuals handle a four-pack of toilet paper varies, depending on levels of organizational outlook and habits. Perhaps how you deal with toilet paper when you first buy it corresponds to your personal level of organizing in other areas.

When you buy toilet paper, what do you do (check one)?

____ Leave it in the car and then bring the package into the house when needed.

____ Leave the pack sitting in the kitchen when the groceries are unpacked.

____ Throw it down the hall toward the bathroom or storage spot.

____ Put the package in the bathroom or storage area, opening the package when the first roll is needed and later struggling to get each roll out of the wrapping as needed.

____ Unwrap the pack so that individual rolls are easily available and distribute them to individual bathrooms or near where they will be needed.

Of the five, the last one is the kindest to yourself. Taking the time initially to put the toilet paper where it is accessible makes life easier. It is doing this kind of small deed consistently that keeps a person on top of things. In the end it makes life simpler so you don't spend your time catching up, sending someone out to the car, or always looking for things.

Managing Your Time and Life

Time Management the Low-Tech Way

If you don't know where you're going, you can't get there! Therefore, visualize and then write down how you would like to use your time, articulating your priorities and goals. Whenever an idea or task presents itself, determine how it meshes with these priorities and goals. If it's something you want/need to do, ask yourself the magic word: "WHEN?" Then enter into your tickler or planner when you plan to begin and complete the item, even if it's months away. Now it's not one of those free-floating anxiety-producing thoughts, and it won't slip through the cracks (unless you don't look at your tickler or planner)! If you can't do it when it comes up in your system, move it. If you have to move it several times, consider whether it truly meshes with your priorities and goals.

Ann W. Saunders
S.O.S.—Simple Organizing Solutions
Baltimore, Maryland
www.SOSforOrganizing.com

Power Organizing the High-Tech Way

Make your computer the central hub for all of your phone contacts, fax and letter correspondence, to-do lists, addresses, reminders, and calendar information. With personal information manager (PIM) software, such as Outlook, Act, Entourage, and Goldmine, you can do all that and even keep track of your email. And the great thing is you only have to enter contacts once. The information in your contact database links to your PIM email, calendar, reminders, to-do lists, and correspondence features. Have your PIM launch automatically by placing it in your start-up folder. If you are on the road a lot, synchronize (hot-sync) your information to your personal digital assistant (PDA) and take it with you. Using a PIM is a great way to stay organized and can help make possible the illusive paperless office.

Do'reen Hein
DoHein@mac.com

"American workers are slaves," said my seatmate on the Lufthansa plane returning to America. He was a man of imposing stature and authoritative accent, an executive with a tire company that had factories in both Germany and America. "They work too long, too hard, and often for too little pay."

I was shocked and a little hurt to hear my hardworking countrymen called slaves. Later as I thought about it, I concluded his perspective had allowed him to clearly identify a problem in American life. It applies not only to work-related experiences but to life in general.

Americans put a very high premium on accomplishments. People are talking faster, driving faster, and packing their schedules with activities back-to-back. Many people are no longer comfortable experiencing the joy of the moment with relaxation or family time. They feel guilty when they are not involved in working toward a goal.

We get rewards of various kinds by working hard, some monetary or physical in nature, some related to self-esteem. But there are two problems that occur when we form the habit of working to finish one job just so we can go to another and then another:

- The payoff becomes less satisfying.
- Once we start running, it's hard to slow down.

Unchallenged, this way of life will lead to health problems, among them depression and physical complaints. If you have been living a busy life and been successful but this activity-oriented life has begun to lose its pleasure, you may be ready to make changes.

IN THE TRENCHES WITH SMART HOMEMAKERS

The order of prioritizing has to be SELF, FAMILY, OTHERS. Years ago I heard (from the La Leche League) that the best way to implement prioritizing is NEEDS BEFORE WANTS. Keep these two principles in mind, and you'll be all set. You need to take care of yourself first, because if you don't, you won't have energy to help anyone else. So in effect, taking care of your needs is taking care of others.

Family is next, for obvious reasons, but it's so easy to cast them aside because "they'll understand" while you go help out your neighbors. You must get in the habit of realistically assessing your needs and your family's needs and then figuring out how much energy you have left to give to others.

Then, once you've given all that you've had left over, you're going to have to learn to be hard-hearted and say no. Of course, you'll do this in a polite and friendly manner. "Oh, I just wish that I could, but I'm sorry, I really can't." No excuse is needed, although if you wish, you may mention some other things that you have to take care of. Most people will accept this except for the most persistent neighbor pests. Those who are so rude as to insist that their needs come before yours

don't deserve to have your help—they're not going to help you
when you need them.

What Do You Really Want?

What most of us really want is unlimited time and
energy. There is exhilaration in living a jam-packed life.
Even the stress of overdoing gives us an adrenaline rush
that we grow used to and that feels natural and good
after a while. But our dealings with time and energy
bring us back to the reality of life. We can do only a
limited number of things. To fit in all of the important
ones, we must control our time—or rather ourselves.
Unfortunately, we are forced by reality to make choices
to include some things and (sigh) omit others.

If you feel stressed by having more to do than time or
energy will allow, determine the areas of life over which
you have the most control. Where do you have power to
make decisions that will relieve some of the pressure?
In the list below, put a check by any life responsibilities you can modify. Put two checks by any that need
to be modified badly *or* over which you have the power
to make significant change. Keep these in mind as you
evaluate your activities later in the chapter to find the
parts of your life that have the greatest impact.

____ 1. *Work hours.* Could you spend less time on your
work? Do you stay at work longer than you need
to?

____2. *Commuting time.* Are there any changes you
can make, such as changing jobs, moving
closer to your job, or taking another mode of
transportation?

____3. *Housework.* Is there any way you can spend less
time working on the house? You could ask for

more family involvement or have a friend or professional organizer help you organize for more efficiency. You could hire someone to clean. You could lower your standards or organize yourself and your routine to do things more efficiently.

____4. *Cooking time.* Can you plan better, cook and freeze on the first day of the week, eat out more, bring cooked food in?

____5. *Additional responsibilities.* Do you have responsibilities that you can omit or modify? Perhaps you have too many pets to feed, groom, and take to the vet. You may have overcommitted yourself to help friends. Is your garden or yard too big?

____6. *Hobbies, sports, reading, entertainment such as television.* Most of us can minimize time spent on activities in this area, although this may be the hardest of all. We are an entertainment-hungry society, and entertainment consumes a large part of our time.

____7. *Ministry or charity.* Are the activities you are involved in the best ones for you? Would something else fit in better with your talents and time? Evaluate carefully so your efforts will be the most productive.

____8. *Some other activity that consumes a lot of your time.*

The Bare Bones Way

Life in general, including home life, is becoming more and more frenetic. Everything, including gym time, classes, children's activities, meals, even volunteer service, must be scheduled.

In the past, writers of screenplays used the rule of thumb that one page of dialogue equaled one minute of performance. Now, because people are talking faster, a page of dialogue equals forty seconds. Because of the focus on speed, people seem to be walking, driving, and in general moving faster. Just as we are seeking faster and faster computers, we are seeking to digitize ourselves so we can speed up production and consumption.

For some, the home is so busy and unfulfilling that they seek satisfaction at work as a substitute. Work becomes less stressful than home life, and companionship develops there. Habits develop that cause further neglect of the home.

> Only by stopping and evaluating where we are in fulfilling what is really important to us can we get a handle on how we want to use our time to live our lives.

Only by stopping and evaluating where we are in fulfilling what is really important to us can we get a handle on how we want to use our time to live our lives.

The Heart of Time Management

The heart of time management the Bare Bones Way is deciding ahead of time our chief (top 20 percent) priorities or life goals and limit the bulk of our time, attention, and energy to those. Some priorities last a lifetime; others vary with the seasons of life. Whatever our priorities are, daily decisions must support them, keeping them alive and healthy.

Life goals are like the queen bee in a hive. Daily activities are like worker bees that hover around the queen. Their one desire is to support her however they can. A

Here it is important to remember the KISS principle: *Keep it super simple.*

bee that goes out on its own to do something else is ejected from the hive.

Often we spend time on activities in our lives that have little or nothing to do with our goals. If we want to do less and accomplish more, we need to eject those activities and keep only the ones that move our lives forward to where we really want to go.

Locating the Queen Bees

Obviously the most important part of this is to identify the queen bees of our lives. Identify priorities by making a circle graph. Making a circle graph instead of a list eliminates the problem of having to rank our priorities in order of importance, which is difficult to do and tends to stop us from moving forward with the process. Later you will make some judgments about the place of importance of each of your priorities.

Jot down in any order five or six aspects of your life that are really important to you. Here it is important to remember the KISS principle: *Keep it super simple.* Then make a circle and draw as many pie wedges as you have priorities. This is important because it helps you isolate your priorities in your own thinking.

Most of us will list some of the same things, such as family life, work, personal and spiritual development (some may wish to put God or spiritual development as a circle in the middle that becomes a part of all of the other pieces), and finances. You may want to separate categories in a different way. For example, have a different pie piece for husband, children, and house instead of just calling it family life.

Some things, such as hobbies, pets, sports, or travel, are priorities to one person but not to another. As we

move along in life, our priorities change. Your job right now is to evaluate what is important to you at this time and draw your pie. Don't overdo by making too many pieces. Don't try to do it perfectly; just get it done in a general way so you can move on. If it doesn't distract you, you may wish to number the pieces in order from the most important to the least important. You may wish to write beside the priority how it will work out in your life, for example listing where you want to travel beside your travel priority. Again, the main thing is just to draw a pie that shows your priorities in some way.

Reading about this activity and generally considering it mentally will not substitute for actually getting a piece of paper, back of an envelope, or whatever to make your list and quickly sketch a pie with wedges.

These are your life goals for this time in your life. Sticking with them and not being diverted by unimportant activities is at the heart of the Bare Bones approach.

For some this next optional step may be among the most important. Many times we are hindered in accomplishing what is really important to us by the intrusion of other activities that, though they may be good, are not important at this time. They are pie pieces that do not belong in our current pie. Maybe we got pressured into them or maybe they are left over from a previous time of our life and are not appropriate at this time. If this is true of you, you may find it useful to actually draw pie wedges over to the side of your pie chart, label them, and then cross them out. This is a concrete way indicating that you are removing these activities as goals at this time.

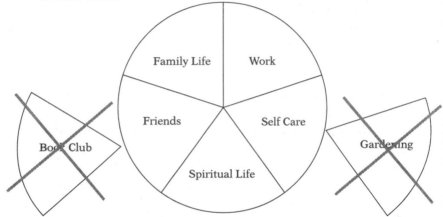

Once you have decided on what is really important in your life, arranging your activities to fit these goals is a necessary but tricky task. All of your activities do one of three things in your life:

- directly support your life goals
- provide background support for your life goals
- interfere with your life goals

Ask yourself the following questions about each activity:

1. *Direct support*. Does this activity directly support my life goals? The goals that do should be adhered

to closely. Being present at children's performances is an example of a direct support for those whose children are a priority. One characteristic of this category is that usually nobody but you can accomplish the goal. If an activity is a key part of a life goal and only you can do it, it is a keeper for sure—a no-brainer.

2. *Background support.* Does this activity provide important background support for my life goals? Organizing the house; shopping for groceries, clothes, and household items; decorating; car care; paying bills; banking; and the like support family life. Dental care, haircuts, and such support self care. These activities are important, even essential, but they should be worked around the activities that directly support your goals. A lot of activities fit into this category. They take up most of our time. A characteristic of this category is that frequently others can do these activities for you. You can delegate, hire workers, or make other arrangements to get the jobs done.

3. *Interference.* Does this activity distract me from my life goals? Rogue activities that don't actively or passively support your life goals need to be jettisoned from your life or at least closely scrutinized to see if they should be omitted.

"To-Don't" List

Dr. Howard Hendricks of Dallas Seminary has said it is obvious none of us can do everything, so we have to make choices. A person has to choose between the things that he or she can do and the things that he or she must do. That calls for elimination. He notes that we all have to-do lists but he suggests we also need to-don't lists.

Do you have five or six items that you are presently doing that should go on your to-don't list, either because you should not be doing them at all or because you can delegate them to somebody else?

At this point, remember the importance of just refusing jobs that don't fit with your priorities. A wonderful little word is *no*. You don't have to explain why you are saying no. It's nice to say, "No, I'm sorry." If pressed, give a general explanation like, "It doesn't fit in with my schedule right now" or "That's just not my style."

Of course, the hardest person to say no to is ourselves. We have many interests, hobbies, and causes to which we want to say yes when we know we don't have the time and it is not one of our predetermined priorities. We must tell ourselves, *Not here, not now—maybe later.* This takes commitment to our predetermined goals.

If your family or coworkers keep wanting you to rescue them, remember the motto that you should post in various places:

Lack of preparation on your part
does not necessarily constitute an emergency
on my part.

If others expect you to respond to problems caused by their poor planning and you cooperate by helping them, you will have a different KISS. You will be kissing your own responsible and productive living good-bye.

Ordering Priorities

Deciding what to do when there are conflicts in scheduling is not always easy. The problem comes when a small problem in a vital area meets a big demand in an unimportant area. This happens all the time in busy lives.

For example, let's assume the following are priorities of a fictional family. They are listed in order, with the most important listed first.

5. *Spiritual development.* Church attendance, family and personal Bible reading at home, participation in church outreach and activities. All of these flow from personal faith.
4. *Family togetherness.* This family has decided that Mom should stay home with the children, the family eats meals together, and Mom and/or Dad go to all sports, school, and other activities of the kids.
3. *Support Dad in his work.* Dad strategizes for promotions. Dad may need to take time for more classes and even consider moving.
2. *Finances.* Plan activities wisely to save for the children's college fund. Will this mean the kids need to get jobs to save money and to study harder to get scholarships? Will it mean less extravagant vacations and forgoing a new car? Review choices of utility companies, insurance companies, and others to see if changes would be beneficial.
1. *Education.* Mom is finishing her college education. The kids may need to pitch in more with cooking and house care.
0. *Other miscellaneous activities.*

Earlier you made a pie chart to begin isolating your priorities. To participate in the next decision making, you will now need to list your priorities in order of the most important down to the miscellaneous activities, which is 0. A 0 means they are not among the top 5 in priority, though they may be important on a daily basis, like feeding and caring for the cats. Don't try to make your list perfect. Just jot down your priorities so you can move forward. Later you can revisit the list and tweak it, adding more if necessary.

5 _____

4 _____

3 _____

2 _____

1 _____

0 _____

Priority Scale

Importance Scale

Does your priority list mean that a church activity that conflicts with a family activity always automatically wins out? No, because some church activities are more inconsequential than others or not as important as activities in a lower priority area. For those who want a formula for making decisions when priorities conflict, try this one. Construct an Importance Scale of 1 to 15, with 15 being very important and 1 very unimportant. For example, on this scale minor emergencies rate a 12, while full-blown emergencies rate a 15.

1	2	3	4	5	6	7	8	9	10	11	12	13	14	15
small issue			somewhat important					definitely important			serious issue			emergency

Importance Scale

Make your decision by using both the Priority Scale and the Importance Scale. It is easy to work this if you think of a balance scale such as elementary school children use when they learn math.

First go to the Priority Scale. Let's say that the church (an important 5 on the Priority Scale) is scheduled to hand out vacation Bible school leaflets in the neighborhood on Saturday afternoon. You are really interested in doing this. However, Grandmother's birthday party (a 4 on the Priority Scale because she is family) is at that time.

Now go to the Importance Scale. Weight the importance of your part in handing out the leaflets. Let us say you decide it is a less important 2. Now weigh your attendance at the party, which you decide is an 8 in importance.

	Leaflets					Grandmother's Party								
1	2	3	4	5	6	7	8	9	10	11	12	13	14	15
small issue				somewhat important					definitely important				serious issue	

Importance Scale

When you add the Priority Scale with the Importance Scale for the church activity, the sum is 7. Add the two for the family activity and the sum is 12. The formula indicates what we already suspected would be true for this family—Grandmother's party is the big winner!

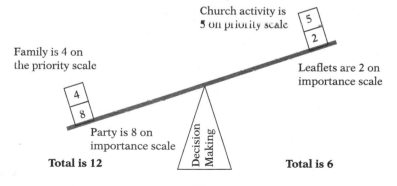

Church activity is
5 on priority scale

Family is 4 on
the priority scale

Leaflets are 2 on
importance scale

Party is 8 on
importance scale

Decision Making

Total is 12   **Total is 6**

The important thing is to clarify the tension you feel in making decisions between what is a general priority in your life and what must be tended to at the moment.

Of course, it may be possible to do both activities, but when you have to choose, weigh the priority and the importance.

In real life, we do not ordinarily make decisions by referring to scales of importance. In our minds, however, we are balancing priorities and importance all the time on a casual basis. When you are just beginning to focus on your priorities or when making hard decisions, a more objective method such as this will help you sort through your thoughts, without being rigid, and keep you committed to what you have decided is really important to your life.

If you use the scale method and strongly disagree with the outcome, go with your personal conviction. Using the scale has helped you clarify how you really feel about your decision, even if the number system did not. The important thing is to clarify the tension you feel in making decisions between what is a general priority in your life and what must be tended to at the moment.

Just for illustration, let's suppose the dog breaks its leg on the afternoon of Grandmother's party. The dog is not on the Priority Scale you have created (not that little Fido is not important!), so the incident is rated 0. But on the Importance Scale the broken leg rates a 15 because it is a serious emergency.

				Grandmother's Party								Fido's leg		
1	2	3	4	5	6	7	8	9	10	11	12	13	14	15
small issue				somewhat important					definitely important			serious issue		

Importance Scale

The dog's broken leg wins over the party, which rated a 12 in the exercise we did before.

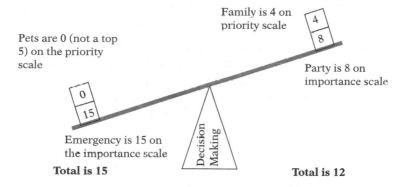

Of course, there are always variables to consider. In this case, some family members could go to the party with your apologies, while you ferry Fido to the vet.

By the way, nobody is going to whip out this book and review the scale (I hope!) to decide whether to go to the party or the vet. This illustration is just to show how the thinking behind the scale works.

Practicalities in the Midst of Priorities

Even though setting priorities and sticking to them provide the framework of a well-ordered life, accomplishing everyday tasks is often where we feel we are faltering in our time use.

Mornings can seem like a leftover nightmare for someone who is less than organized as she bounds out the door, leaving a trail of kids, pets, and discarded clothing in her wake. Here are some ideas on how to set a good tone and get started right at the beginning of the day or the night before. When you plan ahead, the whole day will work better.

1. Do as much as you can the night before. Make the lunches, refrigerating what might spoil. Set the table for breakfast. If you have indecisive kids, have them pick out what they want to wear. If you have trouble making up your own mind, plan what you will wear. Make sure it's clean and ironed.
2. Get the kids to help. A child old enough to go to school is a child who's old enough to help. This means making beds (don't sneak in later to smooth out the wrinkles), packing lunches, buttering toast, clearing the table.
3. Stick to a routine. Make beds, eat breakfast, wash up, brush teeth, comb hair, get dressed, out the door. Whatever order your family settles on, stay with it regularly. You'll find you all move faster.
4. Keep an eye on the time. As you move along in your routine, occasionally remind everyone what time it is, just so it doesn't get to be later than you think. Set a kitchen timer for five minutes before you need to leave.
5. Discourage anything that keeps you from getting out the door. It's true that reading is educational, but memorizing the back of the cereal box doesn't help to keep things moving. Promise to talk over last night's dream at dinner—and then be sure you do it.
6. Try to be sure everybody leaves the house happy. There's nothing worse than picturing those angry faces all day, especially when you can't do anything to set the situation right. A hug and a kiss on the way out the door can make all the difference in your day—and theirs.
7. Make sure the house welcomes you home in the evening. If you will be gone all day, put dinner in a slow cooker so the house is fragrant and dinner is ready when you step in. Leave the living room,

kitchen, and bedrooms in good shape so that you smile when you enter them. Put out potpourri and cut flowers that smile back at you. This is all part of responsible self care.

8. If you do have a bad morning, make things right as soon as possible. If your kids call you after school, that's a good time to say, "I love you. See you tonight."

Basic Tools

TO-DO LIST

Make it easy on yourself by dividing the to-do list into groups. Most people find their groups focus around actions that correspond to four locations:

- around the house, which we will call *do*
- at the phone, which is *call*
- at the computer, which is *write*
- in the car, which is usually *buy*

Fold a piece of paper into four squares by folding it twice, putting the short ends together each time. Label the blocks at the top: *Do, Call, Write, Buy*. In each block, list the activities for the day. Now you have four short, easily analyzed groups of things to do. When you list things in the appropriate box, add pertinent information, such as phone numbers and the like. Finally, put a little box beside each activity you list. Put a check in the box when it is done.

You will notice we have again used the first two Cs of organization. We have consolidated all similar activities into groups, and we have containerized or corralled them under the appropriate heading.

If you find you are overwhelmed by the number of things on your lists, choose just the three most important and make a separate list of these three. Don't look at the longer list until the first three are completely done. Then, if you have time, go back and choose three more.

CALENDAR

Use one calendar to keep track of all your appointments. If you do not need to fit your activities in with the schedules of others, or if they are work-related activities that take place when you are already scheduled to be away from the house, you may wish to use a book or time management scheduler that you carry with you.

If you work your schedule in conjunction with others, say members of the family, use one calendar, and only one, for scheduling. A large yearlong calendar hung on the wall out of public view is easy to use.

SWISS CHEESE METHOD

The Swiss cheese method, which was popularized by Alan Lakein in his classic book *How to Get Control of Your Time and Your Life*, is so useful it must be included with basic tools.[1] If you procrastinate doing a big or unpleasant job, begin to poke holes in it a little at a time. I had a large pile of big photo albums, which I procrastinated moving to another spot until I recalled the Swiss cheese method. Each time I passed the annoying pile, I moved one album into its proper place. Shortly, and I mean very shortly, that pile, which had been there for days, had disappeared.

Quality of Life

If you find that you are busier using these methods, you have missed the point somewhere along the line. You

70

should be less busy, less harried, less stressed because you have more time for vegging, relaxing with family and friends, taking walks, entertaining, reading, hobbies, meditating, and the like.

If the German traveler looked at your life, he should be able to say, "American workers are slaves—but not this guy (or gal)."

Beyond Bare Bones

Here are some ideas for keeping your priorities always in mind. These aren't for everybody—just those who want to go beyond Bare Bones.

- Write your goals in calligraphy and frame them. Do this once a year, maybe at the beginning, to re-evaluate your priorities and determine what is not a priority for you.
- Paint or embroidery your goals onto a piece of fabric and sew them into a pillow cover.
- Draw an Importance Scale, like the one in this chapter, and on the same sheet of paper list your top five priorities in order. Make several copies and have them available when needed for difficult decision making.

Tips

Cut yourself some time slack just by changing a few tactics. Here are some suggestions:

- Live close to places you go regularly, such as your church, dentist, doctor, school, hairdresser, and the like. Each time you change any of these providers, choose ones closer to your house.

71

- Spend less time standing in line by avoiding peak traffic times at stores, banks, and movies. This will take you out of peak times for car traffic as well.
- Do your business with the post office by going to USPS.gov on your computer. Order stamps, track packages, and find zip codes from the privacy of your home. Saves time and energy.
- Take advantage of personalized services, such as pickup and delivery of dry cleaning, online groceries, and restaurants that deliver.
- Employ technology for such things as banking by telephone or computer and online bill payment and movie ticket purchases. Online banking is gaining in popularity, up from fourteen million in 2000 to forty-seven million in 2003.
- Group errands so you accomplish many things in one trip.
- Make appointments early in the day to avoid waiting when the schedule of the doctor or lawyer gets backed up.
- Use your oven timer to find out exactly how long it takes to do jobs you avoid because you don't like them. When you discover that it really takes only five minutes to vacuum the bedroom, you'll be less hesitant about going in there and getting the job done. Many tasks take very little time to do. It's the procrastination that eats up the hours.
- Save time shopping by checking out www.consumersearch. com for opinions on the best products for the best price.
- Store often used articles, like scissors, tape, nail files, and pens, in various corners of the house for easy access.
- Use a headphone for your cordless phone so you can dust, power walk around the house, or whatever while you talk or are put on hold.
- On the road, use the automated toll-pay program where it is available.

Decision Time—Choose Your Top 20 Percent

Since life is an integrated whole made up of things that are important to you, it may not be appropriate to drop all but 20 percent of your priorities. It is appropriate, however, to major on the majors, though minor issues remain in the background. We get in trouble when we major on the minors.

Several practical ideas have been given in this chapter for getting control of your time. Check the ones below that will help you accomplish your priorities.

____ Make a to-do list.

____ Buy a large yearlong calendar and enter all appointments on it.

____ Use the Swiss cheese method on a task that you have been avoiding. Which task is it?

____ Make a change in your tactics, as suggested in the Tips section at the end of the chapter. Which ones will you change?

Getting It Done

The No-Exception Rule

Sometimes significant things in our lives are chronically neglected, like taking vitamins every day or exercising regularly. For these small but important details in my life, I decided to impose the "No-Exception Rule" on myself. As soon as I hear myself thinking of an excuse to put off my stretching exercises or vitamins, I remember the No-Exception Rule and just do it.

The No-Exception Rule offers significant help in organizing our lives as well, not so much in the big things but in the important little ones that trip us up daily if we don't do them. Apply it to things that tend toward inconsistency, things like detrashing the car after each use, making the bed, reading and deleting emails, hanging up coats and clothes, and putting makeup away after it is used.

One caution is necessary. Use this powerful force for only one or two important details at a time. It feels great to make strides in these little areas. Once you conquer the one or two areas you have selected, you may be inspired to move on to applying it later to other small areas or even to larger issues in your organizational life.

I have improved in taking vitamins and stretching from about 50 percent of the time to about 98 percent of the time. The No-Exception Rule has proved very effective in my life. It is definitely a strong influence for change.

Mary Pankiewicz
Clutter Free and Organized
Knoxville, Tennessee
www.clutterfree.biz

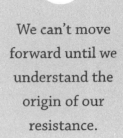

We can't move forward until we understand the origin of our resistance.

The Roots of Disorganization

Disorganization is not always an individual matter. Sometimes the house is just the floor on which we do a dance of disorganization with others. It may be that someone in the house (maybe you) is resisting keeping the house nicer because he or she wants to show anger. An example may be a child who is leaving stuff around the house and not cleaning up the room as a statement of independence or a spouse who leaves things messy as a weapon in a family conflict.

A more subtle example is that deep in your own heart you may be angry about the nature of life that forces you to spend your time doing grunge jobs that you hate. Or maybe you hear the voice of your mom, the neatness police, echoing from the past and you resent it.

Our messy behavior may have deep roots that need to be considered. We can't move forward until we understand the origin of our resistance.

IN THE TRENCHES WITH SMART HOMEMAKERS

From Dianne—Making and Using a Brain Clutter List

A brain clutter list requires about 20 to 30 minutes of as uninterrupted time as you can muster. It is wonderful for getting things done. This list boils down to everything in your head that you think needs to be done immediately and long term. Just get a piece of paper and begin writing everything you think of that needs your attention. I used my PC—seems I go faster if I type it. You list whatever comes to mind from the water bill to the laundry to the storm windows to the kitchen floor to paint your nails to shampoo the carpets to hang that picture to clean out that closet to make out your will—whatever. *All* of it. Don't think in terms of today, tomorrow, or next week. Just sit and begin listing everything you need to attend to! The miniscule tasks to the big tasks will come to mind, and you need to put them all down. JUST GET IT OUT OF YOUR BRAIN AND ON TO THE PAPER. You'll be amazed at what comes to mind. Don't let it overwhelm you. You are listing these things, not getting up to worry over them and do them right now.

When you are done, breathe, breathe deeply! Relax. This is so very important to relay to you! I highly suggest you don't really look at the list when you are done. Set it aside. Wait a day or two before doing step two.

Step two is looking at the things you wrote down and giving them some kind of time in your life. I work best if I don't try to overdo scheduling. The simpler the better for me or I get all caught up in the scheduling and I don't get anything done.

I use Post-it notes and I slap one on each of the monthly calendar pages of my main wall calendar. For instance, my porch needs to be stained. This has been on my mind forever. Well, I am finally putting it away in its proper place now. I will do that next April! Done and over with. I release that to April of next year. And you know, I feel soooo much better about that particular task now, and if I even begin to let the thought creep in that I will . . . nope. That is in *April*! :) Good, very good feeling!!

I think a brain clutter list is so refreshing! It helps me so much to GIVE certain things to the future so that I can zone in on the present. This acknowledgment of things and then the giving of them to a time later helps me relax about today. And if you whisper a prayer to the Lord about certain things that are really getting to your gut, he will indeed help you!

From Della:
I have arrived. For now I can visualize in great detail for the first time the other phases of this project: Sort and file my papers; destain and repair and hang up my clothes; convert my second bathroom into a library lined with bookcases; sort my possessions into permanent possession boxes with labeled categories and place on shelves around abode; paint my walls, in pretty, already-picked-out colors; decorate.

Now those phases don't seem like work at all. They seem simple and easy, because I have come over the mountain. I have reached the summit and planted my flag, saying: "Hey, world. Here I am." And it will be all coasting from here.

From Carol:
I never learned nor had a feel for what should be thrown away and what should be kept. I was afraid of throwing something out because I was sure that as soon as I did, I would need it. I still have a problem with tossing metal juice lids from frozen juice cans, and bottled water bottles. It took a LONG time to get to that point (but I did!).

I felt overwhelmed and powerless—mentally frozen and physically exhausted just thinking about it. I just couldn't bring myself to deal with doing all this cleaning and decluttering. It was too much for me, so I avoided it by "scrubbing cracks with a toothbrush" to make myself feel that I accomplished something while ignoring the real problem.

From Ella:
You don't have to do it "right" the first time. Housework done poorly is better than housework not done at all. Only the perfectionist in us has to have it done perfectly. Waiting until I

could get it done perfectly or right is what got me so far behind in the first place.

The Bare Bones Way

Once you have your priorities in mind and are willing to face making changes, *do sweat the small stuff.*

As you know, like us, police have priorities. How they handle them will teach us much about accomplishing our goals. Using the pyramid as an example, the police place quality-of-life issues on the bottom. They are issues like noise, graffiti, urinating in public, broken windows, and the like. More serious crimes are obviously more important.

However, a strange thing happens when police pay attention to the "unimportant" little things on the bottom of the pyramid. Fascinating studies have shown that when small matters are not attended to, people think nobody cares about the neighborhood or the behavior of the people in the neighborhood. Once they get that idea, other breaches follow naturally. Somehow, keeping on top of the small things makes crime go down.

There must be a principle in there somewhere, because the same thing happens with housekeeping. When we attend to the little things consistently, the big things follow in the right direction consistently. When we let little messes begin, disorder avalanches behind them.

For those of us who struggle with organization, order can unravel quickly. Why does it work that way? The answer has to do with the concept of breach of integrity. A little something wrong destroys the effect of the whole thing.

Think of it this way. If a beautiful model, dressed in designer clothes and carrying herself elegantly, smiles at you and reveals a missing front tooth, the whole effect is ruined. A dam holds back the water until a small hole appears. That small hole is not going to remain small. The flow of water will widen it until the whole dam is ruined. The same is true with the house. If you have prepared a lovely living room for company, complete with flowers and shining surfaces, a dirty sock on the floor ruins the whole effect.

It is much easier to keep the whole thing working well than to keep repairing it.

In a similar way, once a person develops a system for organizing the house, if one part of the system begins to crack, the whole plan is in danger of disintegration—at least until the crack is repaired. And repairing cracks again and again is exhausting. It is much easier to keep the whole thing working well than to keep repairing it.

This "keeping it together" is called maintenance.

Choose Your Details Wisely

The people who keep on top of things are those who take care of the right details properly and on time. It is essential for maintenance. In the mountain of important factors that maintain organization, this tip is one of two or three that rises above the clouds

Don't be misled. I am not talking about perfectionistic attention to doing things without flaw. Just the opposite. Just do "it." But make sure the "its" you are doing are the significant ones.

IMPORTANT SEQUENTIAL DETAILS

Taking care of details is not as simple as it seems. Grandma's adage, "A stitch in time saves nine," was a clever little rhyme that aimed at this principle. But, like all quickie sayings, it left out some fairly important considerations.

Let's consider how it worked for her. Grandma did hand sewing. She could easily see that if a knot came loose in her needlework and the thread started to unravel due to pressure or whatever, it would not be long before the whole seam would pull open. If she had just caught that first stitch before it unraveled, she would have saved herself the work of stitching up the whole seam. So Grandma was reminded as she sewed day by day to keep up with the details of maintenance.

Good for Grandma. It probably worked great for her, but that is not the whole story. All stitches are not created equal. Some details are important. Others are not.

The ones that are important are the ones I call important sequential details. Like the stitch Grandma was so fixated on, these details are part of a bigger project. Making the bed is important because it is a significant part of the larger project of having a nice looking bedroom. Unloading the dishwasher in a timely fashion will keep the dirty dishes from having to back up in the sink. Handling the mail quickly keeps piles from forming. Those are all stitches in time.

In addition to these regular details that keep things moving smoothly forward are little unexpected but important details. Housekeepers who never seem to be working at cleaning or organizing are masters at these. Like a mongoose after a cobra, they are always on the alert for an offending mess to eliminate. A piece of fluff is on the rug, they dip down and pick it up on the way to the kitchen. A stain on a blouse? They give it a quick spray of stain remover. They stay on top of things so it appears that they never work. In reality, they don't work much because they have the house and their habits so under control that tidiness moves forward with a minimum of moment-by-moment attention. What they do not do is hop from one unnecessary detail to another as it catches their attention or comes to mind.

UNIMPORTANT RANDOM DETAILS

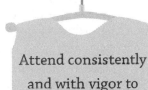

Attend consistently and with vigor to important sequential details.

Details that are not important for overall maintenance are things like keeping used slivers of soap to melt them into liquid soap; ungluing an empty favorite decorator tissue box, refilling it with new tissues, and regluing it (I am not making this up); keeping, storing, and categorizing empty plastic butter tubs—and, of course, their matching tops. These, and all details like them, are not part of a larger plan. To do them does not make any significant contribution to the organization of the house. They are unimportant random details that would best be left undone. Such things as straightening silverware, organizing and alphabetizing CDs, cleaning in too much detail, decorating or working on crafts when the house needs attention. These distract you away from your overall goal. They take unnecessary time and sometimes space that does not contribute to the overall beauty or order of the house.

Like Carol who scrubbed cracks with toothbrushes to avoid more demanding but significant jobs, many women spend time attending to these unimportant random details, thinking they are doing the right thing. In the back of their mind, they wonder why they are working so hard and have so little to show for it. It's because they are doing jobs that are not part of the important 20 percent.

Stop attending to that kind of detail in your life. Attend consistently and with vigor to important sequential details.

DAILY DECISION MAKING

"Ah!" you may say, "but how can I know which are the right details, the 20 percent that is important to attend to?" The answer has to do with awareness of the place of the detail in the overall organization plan. Two key points are that any detail should be visually significant and part of a larger organization plan.

To decide if a detail is *visually significant*, ask the following questions:

- Does neglecting this detail bring public embarrassment? For example, removing dirty laundry or recycled plastic bags from the foyer or the living room is a priority.
- Does neglecting this detail hurt organizational morale? Dead flowers in a vase in the bedroom are demoralizing and should be removed quickly.
- Is it insignificant as far as making a visual impression? Paying attention to neatly lining up shoes in your closet or carefully placing jewelry in a jewelry box do not make a visual impression and so are not significant.
- Does the detail serve to inspire you? A clean sink, a rapidly emptied dishwasher, a shining coffee table, a beautifully made bed, while not significant in themselves, carry a heavy weight because they are able to keep us motivated.

If a detail is not a *part of a larger organizational plan*, it should not be given high priority. Ask the following questions:

- Does neglecting this detail hold up the organizational flow? Misplaced car keys hinder moving forward. Setting up a spot to keep keys and developing the habit of putting them there are priorities.

- Does neglecting this detail cause chronic stress? Perhaps clean laundry piles up unfolded (or folded) in the living room. To relieve stress, change the system and the place for handling laundry.

- Is the detail part of a larger important picture? Maintain the integrity of the whole operation of a well-organized and beautiful house by keeping on top of any details that if neglected would distract from the beauty and order of the house. Sometimes this will mean attacking a hot spot of clutter or putting away a pair of shoes. Sometimes it will mean wiping an unsightly smudge off the front door. There are a lot of little things that can be done but don't contribute to maintaining the well-kept home. Learn to focus only on the significant ones. You know the principle. Spend time only on the top 20 percent that will really make a difference, either for getting the house organized or keeping it in order. The insignificant 80 percent can be ignored forever, given a lick and a promise, or put off till later. That is the Bare Bones Way.

Decision Time—Choose Your Top 20 Percent

Are there any details to which you need to attend?

- Choose one area of your home where you can improve the visual impact. Often the best place to start is in some public area, such as the entryway. Name that point and what you are going to do about it. I will:

- You need to identify whatever keeps holding you up and frustrating you, such as lost keys, empty condiment jars in the refrigerator, or missing pens and paper at the telephone. (See below for a resource to help find things.) Or perhaps it is something that is hard to access, such as the vacuum being upstairs in the closet when you use it downstairs most often. Choose one area that needs to work better and set up a system to correct it.
I will:

- Finally, attune yourself to some little miscellaneous thing that has bothered you but has not been addressed. Maybe it is something broken that needs to be fixed. You may have become used to it that way. You could fix it easily yourself but haven't. Or you need to get somebody else to take care of it. Perhaps it is something that needs to be returned and has been sitting by the front door or in the garage for too long. You are stymied because you don't have the receipt or you don't know if they will take it back. Call and find out. If you can't return it, give it to charity. Begin to take care of these little things today.
I will:

Resource: If you consistently lose keys, television remotes, a favorite toy, or cell phone and spend frustrating hours looking for them, purchase a paging system invented by Sharper Image, called "Now You Can Find It!" It will electronically beep for up to four tagged items when you come within thirty feet of the lost thing. Contact SharperImage.com or 1-800-344-4444.

6

Consistency— The Secret of Maintenance

Strategies for achieving the most valuable results in life include "routinizing the routinizable." Figure out the most efficient way of doing something that must be done regularly, and then do it that same way every time, and at the same time every day or week (or month or quarter).

Examples:

Laundry loads on certain day(s) of the week.
Grocery shopping on certain day(s) of the week.

Learn the layout of your primary supermarket and arrange
shopping list accordingly to pick up all items without
backtracking.
Bring mail into the house and sort for action later; discard
junk mail immediately.

Benefits of routines:

No need to repeatedly decide how/when to do something
(saves nervous energy).
Feeling that things are under control.
More energy available to deal with non-routine demands.

From William Oncken Jr.
Managing Management Time (Prentice Hall)
Monica Silver, Professional Organizer
Tucson, Arizona

There is a group of neat people who never seem to
have a messy house or spend much time cleaning up
messes. They maintain their homes on an even keel. How
they do this puzzles those of us who tend to experience
messes even though we constantly battle them. How do
our friends do it? They are the epitome of a Bare Bones
housekeeper, because they seem to put forth little effort
and yet get maximum benefit.

When we testily feel the need to justify our own struggles in this area, we may mentally accuse them of being
boring people who don't deal with exciting experiences
that pull them into disorder as we do. We agree, quietly
and politely, of course, with the motto, "A clean house
is a sign of a dull life."

If we look carefully, their secret is readily revealed.
They practice the fourth C—continue—which follows
the preparatory three Cs—consolidate, containerize,
condense. They do continuous incidental cleaning and
straightening. Or to put it another way, they get the

house in order and "continue" to follow habits that keep the house organized.

Some of us neglect maintenance. As a result, our houses tend to be in chronic disarray, or we set aside blocks of time (which we may or may not use) to "do housework."

Staying on Top of Things

Those who practice incidental continuous cleaning and straightening as the backbone of their housekeeping enjoy a neat house pretty much all the time. Strangely enough, often they don't recognize what they are doing. If you ask them, they will tell you they don't spend much time on the house. They have better things to do. They don't count their stay-on-top-of-things approach as a housekeeping method.

But it is. It really is. In truth, it is the most powerful maintenance method in existence.

Those who practice incidental continuous cleaning and straightening as the backbone of their housekeeping enjoy a neat house pretty much all the time.

Characteristics of Organized People

But how do they do it? How can they work so effortlessly and yet so successfully? Careful observation uncovers seven characteristics that organized people possess. They are visually sensitive, aware of needs, keep up with details, are organized for work, don't procrastinate, have a consistent focus, and follow a routine. Build these seven characteristics into your life, and your house will always be maintained! That's a promise!

Let's look at them in a little more detail.

- Consistently organized people have a visual sensitivity about what is out of place, and it bothers them. The less organized group either doesn't notice or it doesn't bother them very much. At least they try to ignore it.

- Consistently organized people are aware of little things that need to be done. If they have a moment or two, they draw on that awareness and change the blown out lightbulb, vacuum the rug, or touch up their nails. The other group would be willing to do these things, but when they have a spare moment, they don't remember that the bulb is out or their nails are ragged.

- Consistently organized people don't mind doing little jobs and piecemeal projects. Less organized folks are often philosophically committed to doing only big projects, so they ignore things needing to be done until the designated cleaning time for the area comes (if it ever does).

- Consistently organized people have houses that are prepared for jobs. Their tools and products are readily accessible. The other group doesn't quite recall where all of the cleaning products are located, and the vacuum, mop, bucket, and the like are too hard to retrieve for doing a job easily.

- Consistently organized people don't allow much time to pass between what needs doing and doing it. Others dawdle a little (or maybe more than a little) before getting to the tasks.

IN THE TRENCHES WITH SMART HOMEMAKERS

From Judy:
I have taken on the habit of cleaning my dishes NOW. It is really nice not to have them pile up. I really challenge keeping the

sink clean. I am very proud of myself for doing this. My kids
are even noticing it.

- Consistently organized people keep a consistent
  focus. They have strong boundaries in their lives and
  time use. They know what they want and they don't
  allow others to take over their goals or schedules.
  Others who are "flexible" drop their plans for some
  other opportunity or to help others.
- Consistently organized people have a routine. Sometimes they don't even realize it or call it a routine. To
  them it is just common sense to keep things moving forward in a regular pattern of behavior. Less
  organized folks make decisions on a case-by-case
  basis depending on how they feel, how much time
  they have, and the like.

If we wish to share in the success of consistently organized people, we will have to pick up some of their characteristics, which will lead us to maintain things the way
they do and keep up with clutter as we go.

What You Really Want

Without taking time for serious thought, choose one
or two statements from the four sentences below that
best states your feelings about what you want.

____ I want to be a capable, can-do person who
finally gets on top of the problem of clutter.

____ I want to be competent. Competent means
"adequate" to do the job.

____ I want to be effective. That means I am able
to accomplish the desired effect.

___ I want to be efficient—productive without waste. I want to get the job accomplished with the least effort possible.

All of these statements may seem desirable, but one or two will best state what you want. Once you are specific about your desires, you can hone your actions toward that goal and, more important, de-emphasize goals that are not truly important to you.

IN THE TRENCHES WITH SMART HOMEMAKERS

I'm so excited about progress—it seems to get better every day at our house. A couple of helps I have found:

1. Keep wastebaskets handy and empty often!
2. I invested in printer paper for the computer that has the holes punched in it—I don't put computer info, emails, or ideas anywhere but my notebook. Then I highlight special ideas—at the end of the month I go back and ruthlessly remove much—keep important stuff in chronological order or by topic.
3. I like to make a project of disposing of ten things at a time. When I see a pile or messy area and the old panic feeling comes, I say out loud, "Pick up the top thing and put it where it belongs—preferably the trash!" As I do that one thing, the next one seems easier—Then I say "OK, only ten things this time," then leave the area!
4. My husband and I have agreed to pay for one extra garbage can pickup per week until the house is clean! Keep on working and encouraging!

The Bare Bones Way Action Steps

You already have habits. If your house is still drifting into clutter, the habits you have aren't moving you in the right direction. Assuming your house is reasonably organized and ready for maintenance, you need to re-place the old habits by working the following three new habits slowly into your life.

1. Make a morning and an evening daily routine and follow them.
2. Introduce one new habit at a time.
3. Commit to a fifteen-minute cleaning routine once or twice daily.

The *first action step* is to develop a morning and an evening daily routine and follow them. Use the Four-Plus-Four Bare Bones Plan explained below.

- Write down four things to do every morning. Include making the bed and getting fully dressed as two of the four.
- Write down four things to do each night. Prepare for getting off to a good start in the morning by doing such things as making lunches, laying out clothes, and putting things you will need the next day by the door.
- Post your plan in an easily visible spot. This simple plan will change your life.

IN THE TRENCHES WITH SMART HOMEMAKERS

The thing that has helped me stay on track is routines. I know it sounds dull and boring, but I have added a few things to my morning and evening routines and voila! I just do them without thinking. I follow Sandra's list: get up, make up the bed, etc. After taking care of myself for a couple of months, I did another important thing: I helped my 4 yo DD [4-year-old dear daughter] make a list of *her* morning routine. I let her choose pictures (from a small selection) and wrote beside it what it was. We hung it inside the closet, and I have her look at it

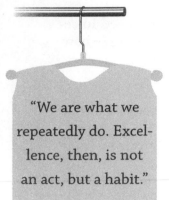

> "We are what we repeatedly do. Excellence, then, is not an act, but a habit."

every morning. After we finished it, my husband said he thought it would be helpful for grown-ups, too. DD has had her list for 2 weeks and hardly refers to it but knows what to do. We're going to make a night routine next.

We move to our new home in 4 weeks. I'll do one for my husband then, too.

The *next action step* is to introduce one new habit at a time. You already live your life using many habits. Procrastinating is a habit. Walking away and leaving something on the counter is a habit. Doing only big jobs and ignoring small ones because they are not worthwhile is a habit.

We don't break habits. What we do is replace them with new habits that are incompatible with the unproductive habits. Initially this is done solely by an act of the will. We feel uncomfortable when we first begin doing something different, but we keep it up because somewhere along the way we have realized that these old habits are interfering with the lives we have now determined we really want to live.

If we have a habit of shopping or going to garage sales and bringing home what becomes clutter in our homes, we need to replace that habit with some other activity, perhaps social get-togethers or a satisfying hobby of some other sort. Aristotle stated the fact well when he said, "We are what we repeatedly do. Excellence, then, is not an act, but a habit."

Let's simplify, as we are inclined to do in the Bare Bones Way. Let's narrow it down to only five habits, the most important ones that will bring the greatest reward, and focus on only one at a time. Choose one of these habits, post it in an obvious place, and begin to do it at every opportunity.

Do it only one day at a time. When the next day arrives, recommit to the same habit until it is more or less automatic. As that one habit becomes a part of your life, choose another one to work on.

1. *If you get it out, put it away.* Or to expand on this habit a bit further: *Put away what you get out as soon as you are finished with it.* If there is one habit and only one that you could embrace for an orderly life, this would be it.

I was talking to Jeff, a young man whose wife is an invalid. He works full-time, cooks, cleans, cares for his wife, does the yard work, is active in church ministry, and has a reputation for keeping an immaculate and orderly home. As he stood behind a table handing out brochures related to his church, I asked him to think about what secret he had for his orderly home and get back to me when he had thought of one, but he didn't have to ponder his answer. He was so intent on what he was saying that he leaned across the table to make sure I could hear clearly in the hubbub of the room. "Always put back immediately what you get out" was his word to me.

Profound insight? No. Powerful information? Yes.

His wife calls this continually moving things back to where they belong "the process of elimination." It definitely eliminates clutter.

Putting things away as soon as you finish with them is the key. Don't do it some time in the future. Do it in a timely fashion. Planning to put the item away later does not substitute for actually doing it. Don't put it close to where it should be. Deposit it exactly where it came from. This one habit, consistently followed, will revolutionize many households.

2. *Apply the thirty-second rule.* If it takes thirty seconds or less to do something, do it immediately. Put packages

93

where they belong. Hang up clothes. Pick up the towels and put dirty clothes in the bathroom hamper. Return the garbage can to the backyard. Clear the table. Gather and throw away trash from the car.

3. *Follow the camping rule.* Leave the area in the condition you found it or better. When you leave an area or room, look back and focus on seeing what you have left behind.

4. *Look, really look, at your surroundings.* Naturally organized people are visually astute. If it's not second nature for you, train yourself to tune in to how the house looks. You will be surprised at what you see that before did not catch your attention. As you declutter so that there are more clear spaces, things that are out of place will become more obvious.

5. *Use spare minutes.* Whenever you have a minute or two, do a little something. Dust, pick up something and put it away, file a paper, replace a burned out lightbulb. These are things that can be done in a jiffy. When you walk through a room, look for anything out of place and make a quick alteration. Make this habit a part of your overall program and the house will stay orderly as if by magic.

The *final action step* is to commit to a simple fifteen-minute cleaning routine once or twice daily. If you follow the Four-Plus-Four Plan and slowly change your habits, you are well on the way toward having the house you want without a lot of work. But even when these two action steps are followed, things ooze out and need to be caught up on a regular basis.

To remedy the situation, set aside fifteen minutes by the timer in the morning and in the evening to maintain your home. This should keep it looking nice, according to the Bare Bones Way. Be sure to include your family in this endeavor.

You may think this is impossible. Maybe, but don't knock it till you try it. Many, many women (and probably guys too) into whose well-kept houses you go spend fifteen or so minutes in the morning to clean up and fifteen in the evening to straighten up. Then they call it quits. This does not include meal preparation time, laundry, or paperwork, like bill paying. But for having an orderly house, this approach will do the trick.

Of course, if your standards are high or your house is large, you may need more than fifteen minutes twice a day. If necessary, add a bit more time to keep things the way you want them.

IN THE TRENCHES WITH SMART HOMEMAKERS

Isn't it amazing how quickly things can be done if we make up our mind to do them? I find that the 15 min. slots take care of several things in a row. If anyone had told me when I started to really deep clean my house what could be done in 5 min., I'd have thought they were daffy.

We let things get bigger in our mind than they really are. We think, Oh I can't start on that now. It'd take too long. And then when we get to it, we find it wasn't the monster we thought. It has made keeping the house in order and organized so much easier. I'd have never started if I hadn't have tried the timer. After that it was so easy just to keep going.

Now, some deep down hard cleaning jobs do take longer. We all know that. Like washing down the walls or shampooing the carpet, big jobs take longer but we know that, so we schedule them for when we know we will have the time to finish, once we start.

But I am so thankful Sandra discovered the time limit way. I think it's one thing that has kept people on the road to recovery.

Maintenance becomes a way of life built on a package of alert attitudes and actions.

Enjoy your trip to recovery and don't rush. You want to do it right the first time, the deep down decluttering and getting rid of stuff. But you will come back and do some areas again and each time it's easier and quicker to let go of stuff we thought we just had to keep.

Find Your Personal Balance

You alone determine the level you want to maintain. Obviously, there is a reasonable balance. You don't want dirt or clutter to be a problem. You want things to look good and work well, but you don't need perfection. Settle on a range that is acceptable to you. Once you do that, don't settle for less.

Maintenance becomes a way of life built on a package of alert attitudes and actions. Keeping on top of things regularly is an integral part of long-term success. An interesting public safety department study was done by Goldstein concerning community quality of life. The conclusions were discussed earlier and are mentioned here in relation to details in maintenance. He found that when order in the community was allowed to deteriorate even a little, it continued to unravel badly.

Another study by Wilson and Kelling called "Broken Windows" in a 1982 issue of *Atlantic Monthly*, says, "At the community level, disorder and crime are usually inextricably linked, in a kind of developmental sequence. Social psychologists and police officers tend to agree that if a window in a building is broken and is left unrepaired, all the rest of the windows will soon be broken." It goes downhill from there. Crime soon follows.

I don't think we need to worry about the crime part of the study occurring in our houses, but isn't it interesting what a bad effect disorder had? The study goes on to say: "One unrepaired broken window is a signal that no one cares."

You need to keep a certain level of order in your home or you signal to yourself and others in the house that nobody cares. In a maintenance situation, a few things out of place say that it's okay to be messy, and from that point clutter gets worse. However, when you keep the house in order, you are saying that order is important. This message perpetuates more order.

IN THE TRENCHES WITH SMART HOMEMAKERS

From Doreen:

I've used the timer method pretty effectively. I call it the 21/7 method. I belong to a book club and often feel guilty if I'm reading a book instead of cleaning/picking up. If I'm cleaning/picking up, I feel guilty that I'm not doing something I enjoy like reading. The 21/7 method is the compromise. I set the stove timer for 21 minutes and read. Then I set the time for 7 minutes and clean/pick up. When I'm overwhelmed, this method really works!! It helps with my reading too. Depending on the book, I tend to get sleepy if I read too long. The 7 minutes that I'm cleaning is a good break and gives me opportunity to ponder/digest what I just read.

From Jennifer:

The neatest thing has been to be able to maintain a clean area. Once I spent a few hours on it. The kitchen is clean, dishes are washed shortly after meals, laundry is washed in a timely fashion, the stairway to the 2nd floor is cleared of "stuff," the sofa can be used for sitting (not piles), horizontal areas are free to gather dust (not piles) if I choose to let them (!!) and etc. Maintaining takes only a FRACTION of the time compared with decluttering and deep-cleaning (not the dirt kind, the "stuff" kind).

It is so freeing that I have no desire to gloat about it or show it off; I am just enjoying the freedom immensely!

Someday you may be the person mentioned at the beginning of the chapter who doesn't seem to do much but always has a lovely home. The way the house looks makes you happy to walk out into the living room in the morning. It makes you happy to come home at night. You love to invite people in. Your heart leaps up because your home fits your tastes, and it comforts your soul and body.

Now you know the "secret" of successful housekeepers. Be consistent with continuous and incremental maintenance, good habits, a regular routine, and two fifteen-minute daily obligations, one in the morning and one in the evening. Nobody can do for you what you can do for yourself when you use the Bare Bones maintenance method. After a while it will be automatic to you, and you will not even realize why your house stays so nice.

Tips for Maintaining Order

Here are some ideas on how to maintain your home in the condition you love:

- Make a deal with a friend, who is also working on maintaining order, that you will drop over once a week between certain hours on an undetermined day. And she will do the same for you. She will show you around the house. Perhaps you two can have a checklist of important areas you are maintaining or working on. You can discuss habit changes. Knowing someone may drop in does wonders for motivation and focus. Use your computer calendar to remind you of your routine.
- Post the habit you are working on. Teach it to the family. Sing it; draw pictures of it. In short, really spotlight it.

Decision Time—Choose Your Top 20 Percent

This chapter deals with the heart of maintenance—consistency.

Choose one of the five new habits (1. If you get it out, put it away; 2. Apply the thirty-second rule; 3. Follow the camping rule; 4. Look, really look, at your surroundings; 5. Use spare minutes). Which of the five habits would make the biggest difference in your life?

After the first habit is chosen, in what order would you want to approach the other habits? List them in order here:

Consider the Four-Plus-Four Plan (committing yourself to doing four things every morning and four things every evening). If you were to put this into effect, what four things would you do in the morning?

What four would you do at night?

Do you have a timer or some way to time fifteen-minute blocks? (Some people call it the Fifteen-Minute Frenzy.) Will you begin this practice?

Part 2

Working the Plan

7

Living Rooms, Bathrooms, and Beyond

Spotlight on Surfaces

Clearing the surfaces of the house is a powerful organizing tool. When you look at a decorating magazine, the main difference in those houses and what you may see in yours is the conspicuous lack of clutter on surfaces. This includes knick-knacks, trinkets, papers, photos, and the like.

When I first go into a house, I clear the floor of papers, shoes, clothes, toys and whatever else I find there that is out of place and put them in or near where they belong. Then I clear the next lowest surface nearest to the floor. That may be a footstool, a low table, or chair and clear those surfaces.

Next we move up to the next highest surfaces, which may be tables, tops of televisions, or bureaus.

When we start doing difficult surfaces like counters and tables, I start at the right and move left. If necessary, I divide the surface into quadrants, clearing and wiping one quadrant completely before moving on. As I am taking things off, I say aloud where the item goes whether I am alone in my own house or working with someone in theirs.

Quadrant by quadrant, surface by surface, the job is done. The whole emphasis is on creating the visual impact of cleared surfaces. Every time you look back at what you have done, you see significant progress shining from the cleared surfaces.

Marsha Sims
Sort It Out
Miami, Florida
www.sortitout.net

In this chapter we will consider each main area of the house separately and work on improving each one with good results. The main rooms are where the bulk of our living takes place, where we circulate most. Storage and work areas will be considered later.

Overall, the whole house works together as one. What we do in one room will spill over to some degree into another. How well the storage and work areas are organized will impact the main rooms. It is like one of the handheld puzzles in which we slide one square after another trying to get them in numerical order. Each time one square moves, it affects them all.

Bare Bones Info

Zoning is a key concept when we consider organizing rooms. All rooms benefit from applying the idea, some more than others. Basically, developing zones means that similar items are grouped together in specific sections dedicated to certain activities. Examples would be an entertainment zone, baking zone, toy zone, or grooming zone.

Living Room and Family Room

Living areas vary from home to home. Some people who have a family room use their living room only for entertaining or formal family gatherings, such as opening Christmas presents. Others use it for daily living because they don't have a family room. Whether it is a formal living room or a general family living area, it sets the tone of the house when anyone, including you, enters, because it is usually one of the first rooms you see. You want to decorate this room in a way that makes a statement about you and your family. The style, colors, accessories, and placement of furniture speak volumes.

Other living area zones are the conversation center, electronic entertainment center, display area for interests or photos, games and toys center, reading center, and sometimes storage. The availability of electrical outlets will determine the location of the electronic entertainment center and, if you put it in that area, the computer. The placement of these items will in turn determine where other items will fit.

Is your furniture arranged in zones to meet your needs? As you look around your living areas, ask yourself what few changes (20 percent) could make a significant difference. Do you need to rearrange furniture, get rid of pieces of furniture or accessories, buy furniture or bring pieces from another room or from storage? In most cases, the single most significant step for change is removing clutter and furniture. The more clutter cleared from the surfaces, the better. Adding or removing a large piece of furniture will have the greatest impact on creating an orderly appearance.

Pay attention to your emotions as you evaluate. What annoys you is as important as what makes you happy. Then ask yourself, *If I could do anything, what would I do in this room?*

Tips

- Take lighting seriously. If you don't have room on the floor or tables for lights, hang them from the ceiling.
- Take advantage of night-lights.
- If you find you are overrun with wires and cables, keep them under control by using any variety of systems you can buy at an electronics store or a store that carries household organizing equipment. You will find it helpful to use gummed file labels to identify each wire.

Dining Area

Unlike most other rooms, the formal dining room has a single purpose and is dominated by a single furniture unit, the table and chairs. The table is second only to the bed in impact, because of its size. For that reason and because you can't close the door to the dining room as you can the bedroom, the table is visually important.

In some homes, the focus is on the table and chairs alone. In others, a centerpiece and in some cases a tablecloth add to the ambiance. Most of the time a lighting fixture illuminates the table for dining. The table, chairs, and lighting fixture are the basics of function and beauty.

When there is room, a hutch and buffet are often part of the dining room suite and are invaluable for storage.

Formal dining rooms are used only for meals. But in homes where the dining area is an extension of the kitchen or living room, often the table is a place for paying bills, doing homework, playing games, and, in between, eating meals.

Look at your dining area. Has "extra" furniture, which could and maybe should be removed, crept in? Do you have the right size furniture for the area? Does it make the visual impression you want?

In most cases, the single most significant step for change is removing clutter and furniture.

If you could do anything, what one change would you like to make in the dining area? Sometimes, and perhaps especially in the dining room, an appropriate 20 percent change makes a big difference.

Bedrooms for Adults

Bedrooms are usually pressed into multiple uses. Because they are out of public view, storage overflow from the house, exercise equipment, libraries, and home offices are located there. Using a bedroom for work activities changes its character and reduces the personal comfort it can offer. On the other hand, since the bedroom is the most personal room in the house, rightly used it can comfort us in a way no other room can.

The core furniture of most bedrooms is a bed, dresser, and bedside table. A TV set and telephone are probably there as well. Fit essentials in first and then turn to other considerations.

Because the bedroom has varied uses, you need to decide how you are going to manage the placement of furniture and other items. Ideally the bedroom should not be used as a gym, home office, library, or storage area for extra boxes. Remove anything that you feel you can either live without or put some other place. This may include exercise equipment or bookshelves holding unnecessary books. Get rid of clothes that are worn out or that you no longer wear. Focus on the surfaces of your dresser, bedside table, and any other surface in the room. In true Bare Bones fashion, getting rid of the right few things can make a huge difference in how much room you have.

Maximize storage areas. Under-bed storage containers are available. Can you rearrange your drawers, grouping things together and storing them for easy access? Can you use the closet for storage of things that are now in the bedroom itself?

Look around your bedroom. If you could remove one thing, what would it be? Do you need to change any piece of furniture, perhaps exchange it with something in another room? All surfaces should be as clear as possible. Does the top of your dresser need decluttering? Do you need to buy a jewelry box or segment a drawer for jewelry? Identify one problem you can solve immediately.

Once the bedroom is salvaged for its true calling—a haven for your renewal—set up centers, such as grooming, dressing, reading, or entertainment centers, so that the appropriate items are grouped together. Finally you need to focus on beautifying the room. A lovely bedroom resists clutter.

IN THE TRENCHES WITH SMART HOMEMAKERS

From Adrienne:

Hello all. Today I am going to enter *the* room and for all of you wondering which room that is—it would be the one that has a big king size bed in it, 2 side tables, 2 lamps, a chair, and a television. In 95 percent of the households in America, it would be known as the master bedroom, but in my case, it is otherwise known as the storage building, the office, and the sleeping quarters when you can find the bed. It's funny. There always seems to be room on the bed for hubby and kids, and dog and cats, but none for the mommy!! I am first going to locate said bed and strip the sheets, flip the mattress, and while I have the mattress up, I am going to vacuum underneath the bed. Then I will put all of the boxes (that store everything in this house that doesn't appear to have a home) in the living room for right now. It's like bill paying, robbing Peter to pay Paul. I will then attempt to pick up all of the papers and CDs and DVDs that are on the floor (due to children) and try to find where they belong, and I will trash the papers that do not belong. What fun!! Hopefully, at some point, I will be able to find the carpet that surrounds the room. If I do, then I will vacuum it.

So, my dear friends, I am off. I will check in with you this evening, because of course after the storage room comes the mowing outside. It has to be done today and I can't ask the man with the ace bandage on his knee to push a lawn mower. You dare even suggest it!! He can walk the golf course, but push a mower, please!!

Tips

- Make the bed daily as soon as it is empty. Maybe the rule should be that the last one out makes the bed. Or an alternative is to make your side if you get up first and the other side is still occupied. This has certain problems if the other person thrashes about a lot. Because the bed is the biggest piece of furniture in the house, a messy bed casts a bad shadow over the whole house. A neat bed illumines the whole bedroom and house. The fact that you cared enough to make it sets a good tone for the day.
- Keep a dish or tray for jewelry you wear each day but take off at night. Store other jewelry in a jewelry box, on hooks, or in a drawer divided into sections, using boxes or drawer dividers. Again the motto is simple effectiveness. Make it

easy to keep it neat and easy to access. Don't let it get
tangled and unusable. Take storing jewelry seriously.

- If you need more room under your bed for storage, consider
  lifting the bed with risers (usually about six inches)
  designed and sold for that purpose.
- Rotate your mattress regularly so it will wear evenly and last
  longer.
- Use only one set of sheets, which you wash, dry, and
  replace. This saves having to store linens. People put on
  clean bed linens on an average of twice a month.

Guest Bedroom

Where space is tight, the guest room is often used for
other activities. It may double as a sewing room, home
office, exercise room, or whatever. But when guests ar-
rive, it has got to have a bed and someplace for them
to put their clothes. Follow the example of motels and
provide shampoo, conditioner, and soap (maybe the
same ones you brought home from the motel). Put out
towels and blankets. Make room to hang up clothes in
the closet and try to fix a place for an open suitcase. If
you can, provide a TV, radio, and clock.

If you don't have room for a bed in your guest room,
provide for sleeping in some other way. Obtain a quality air
mattress, which comes with a motor and is easily blown
up, a roll away bed, or best of all, a bed that folds up into
the wall that is often a part of a larger storage unit.

If whatever you do meets your guests' basic needs
and says, "I'm glad you're here!" your guest room is
doing just fine.

Bathrooms

It is especially important to organize the bathroom
using classic organizational techniques. As in solving

every organizational problem, three things are necessary when dealing with bathrooms:

1. Create centers in your bathroom:

- Gather up items that are now in the cabinets and on the surfaces and think in terms of developing zones. Put the smaller items, like makeup, toiletries, hair equipment, together in containers. Store larger things on shelves in groups. Things you use often should be within arm's reach as you stand in front of the sink.
- Organize under-the-sink space or another cabinet for storage of towels, toilet paper, cleaning products, and whatever else will fit. Units that mount to the cabinet floor and pull out like a drawer make accessing these things easier.
- Clear the counter as much as possible. Things you don't use every day should not be on the counter. If you are going to keep bulky items, such as hair dryers, electric curlers, and brushes on the counter, corral them in a basket.
- Clear tub, shower, and windowsill surfaces. Things on these surfaces interfere with cleaning the bathroom quickly and easily. If you must use these surfaces, put the items in baskets, which can be easily moved for cleaning.
- Have several hooks or bars for hanging towels and washcloths. Small children find it easier to use hooks. If you don't have enough towel bars mounted on the wall, try a towel bar that hangs on the door hinge or over the door or stands on the floor.
- Manufacturers are always coming up with some new problem-solving product. When you have a problem, you will probably find a surprise solu-

tion if you keep your eyes open the next time you visit a store that carries household products and equipment.

2. Follow the camping rule of leaving the area the same as, or better than, you found it. The bathroom can get messy quickly if not attended to carefully as it is used.

3. Follow a regular routine for cleaning. Do little wipe ups as you go, but somewhere along the line, soap scum, water deposits, and body dirt and oil require that we bring in the big guns of sponges and household cleaners on a regular basis.

Tips

- If a bathroom is shared by several children and is cluttered with their things, get each his or her own colored basket for toiletries. Each can take it back and forth to the bedroom, leaving the bathroom clear.
- Remove all of the things that are not needed in the bathroom to storage.
- Attach a magnetic bar—often used in kitchens to hold knives—to hold tweezers, nail clippers, scissors, razors, and any other small metal items that would ordinarily be difficult to store and access.
- Keep cleaning supplies for the bathroom in each bathroom so they are easily available.
- Suction cups that attach to tile hold razors, soap, and hooks of various kinds to keep your surfaces clear.
- A caddy in the tub or shower is a must for holding bottles of shampoo and conditioner and even washcloths. Determine the size you need before buying.
- Color code towels and washcloths for each person, so when towels are left lying around, the guilty person is immediately exposed.

- Place an additional spring-loaded shower curtain bar centered above the tub. It can hold excess wet towels as well as clothes on hangers that are drying.
- Keep a container of commercial wipeups impregnated with cleaning solution for a quick wipe and shine.
- To remind children of how you expect the bathroom to look when they leave, post a snapshot of the bathroom in clean condition, write out a checklist for cleanup steps for each person using the bathroom, or use both a picture and a checklist.

If a room isn't set up for success, even a child who wants to keep it organized has trouble.

Children's Rooms

Many parents would say their chief problem is not children's rooms but the children who live in them. That's another story. But, in truth, if the room is organized in a way that works for the child who lives in the room, there is a much better chance that it will stay neat. If a room isn't set up for success, even a child who wants to keep it organized has trouble.

Children's rooms go through three basic metamorphoses, from baby to child to teen. The principles of organizing are the same. A child's room falls easily into zones—toys, grooming, work, entertainment, and sleeping.

Toys

Keep down excess. It is easy to gather too many toys and too much furniture to hold them. Start by sorting toys into groups—puzzles, games, stuffed animals, action toys, dolls, and whatever other groupings are obvious—and putting them into boxes, which you label to make the grouping clear. Have one box available for broken toys and incomplete sets to throw away. Have

111

another for toys that have been outgrown or were never favorites and need to be given away.

Including the children in the decision making is often a good idea. If your child and you have a difference of opinion, place the toys in a separate box. Label it TO BE DECIDED LATER. Once these toys have been put into a box and removed from the room, they tend to lose appeal. After a while, let the child know you will soon be giving the things in the box away. Tell the child to take out anything he or she wants before you dispose of it. Now is the time. Usually the child won't want anything, but knowing it's possible to retrieve an item makes it easier for the child to remove it from the room initially.

If things go well, you will remove about 20 percent of the toys from your child's room, improving your situation by 80 percent. Getting rid of large toys or equipment will give extra benefit.

Once you know how many toys you have to deal with, you can decide how to store them for easy use. Some people divide the toys into thirds. They store two of the groups and rotate them in and out from time to time. This system makes it easier to manage placing the remaining toys in the room and easier for the child to play.

Larger toys can be placed in the closet or out of the room in a storage area. Smaller toys can be stored on shelves, grouped together and boxed, or put in baskets, which are then labeled with words or pictures. Put coloring books, drawing paper, and crayons into drawers.

Avoid toy boxes like the plague. Children will happily throw their toys, large and small, into the box for quick cleanup. Lost puzzle pieces, toy parts, little trucks, broken crayons, and balls drop under the large toys never to be seen again.

FURNITURE

Furniture for the child's room boils down to three basic types: the bed, dresser, and a place for toys or entertainment items. Somewhere in the house, perhaps here, there needs to be a table for studying and working on crafts or hobbies.

The balance of enough furniture for storage and decoration but not so much that it crowds the room is a chronic tension in furnishing rooms of any kind, but it is especially difficult in children's rooms.

You will need to use all of the storage tips you know. Here are some:

- Use containers that are designed to be stored under the bed.
- Buy a bed that has drawers built in.
- Have enough drawers for clothing.
- Maximize closet use so there is no "dead space" under the hanging clothes or up near the ceiling.
- Use baskets, boxes, pullout plastic drawer sets, and whatever else can be placed on shelves to hold toys.
- Install a clothes bar in the closet that is low enough for the child to reach.
- Mount a shelf around the top of the wall about a foot from the ceiling to display trophies and collectible items.
- Remove all of the things not necessary for the child's room, including unused play items. Put them in a basement, attic, garage, or storage room.

ELECTRONICS

In today's world, Mom and Dad need to make careful decisions about what electronics to put in the child's room. Children of all ages are likely to have a radio or a music system of some kind. As they grow older, kids can accumulate a telephone (cordless, cell phone, or corded), television, and computer. If they had a refrigerator and hot plate, they would practically have their own apartment. Realize that being able to isolate oneself comfortably in one's room does not create healthy family life and in some cases can cause serious problems. These choices need to be made carefully.

While we are on the topic of electronics in a child's room, note the comments of Bill O'Reilly, who has written the book *Who's Looking Out for You?* In *Parade* magazine he writes, "An effective parent will not allow a TV or computer in a child's room. This is a dangerous world, and the danger is now inside the house. The exploiters want your kids. You must look out for them. Fight hard."[1]

One study revealed the percentage of rooms of children ages eight through twelve that contained the following electronics items.[2]

Television set—64 percent
VCR player—43 percent
Video game console—42 percent
Telephone—22 percent
Computer—13 percent

As in other rooms, electronics in children's rooms must be placed where there are outlets, which affects the placement of the rest of the furniture. Make a schematic on paper to decide where you are going to place the various zones.

Keeping It Clean

You have dejunked the room, gotten the furniture in place, and have established your zones. The one problem that has not been addressed is the habits of the child who lives in the room. When he or she follows the same five habits recommended for adults (see chap. 2), the room will stay organized.

And who is responsible for teaching those five habits both by training and example? It's the same person who bought the furniture and set up the room so it will run in an orderly fashion. We all know who that is.

IN THE TRENCHES WITH SMART HOMEMAKERS

From Rachael:

I can remember the days when my children were under three, since my oldest hasn't quite reached 7 yet. I would suggest organizing toys into categories. You choose what they play with for the morning/day/week. Then they put all those away and you get the new thing out for the allotted time—afternoon/day/week. Make them clean up before lunch and before dinner.

This child training business takes an awful lot of time that we *could* be doing something else. If your landlords ever dropped by and your house was less than perfect and they were less than understanding . . . well, you have crummy landlords. But just explain that you have been busy teaching your children how to take care of their things and it takes a little longer to get to your own things right now.

Kitchen

A kitchen is an excellent place to apply the principles of zoning. Dishes should be stored near the dishwasher. Pots, pans, and food should be near the stove. Some who bake a lot have a special baking area. Kitchens house other items, such as plastic storage containers, flower vases, and miscellaneous items. The first thing necessary is to group all of these items together and decide where to store them appropriately. When you group them, you will probably see a lot of things you have not seen or used in a long time.

Because the kitchen is the place where women nurture the family with food, it holds an emotional spot in their hearts. This makes us suckers for kitchen excess. Most kitchens overflow with widgets, both large and small, that were bought with hope for better, easier family care. Since hope springs eternal, women find it difficult to get rid of unused kitchen gadgets. To bring the kitchen under control, these useless items must go. As you know, simplifying by getting rid of excess (say maybe 20 percent) is a major step in organizing.

Once the items in the kitchen are well organized and stored, good habits will keep the kitchen clean.

KEEPING IT CLEAN

Organized people seem to pay special attention to keeping pots washed up and put away during the cooking process and cleaning the kitchen quickly after meals. Less organized people tend to drift at these points. The temptation to "soak" grimy utensils can become an excuse to delay cleanup. If you feel you must soak something, set the kitchen timer as a reminder to return to the cleanup process shortly and finish up that grimy thing. I've known things to sit hopelessly for days because the pot needed elbow grease, not more soaking. I won't say in whose house I have seen this tendency because of the Fifth Amendment.

As a rule of thumb, when cleaning the stove top after cooking (you do plan to do that, don't you?), let the cleaning solvent sit for half a minute or so to use its magical qualities to the max. That is not "soaking" and is considered not only acceptable but wise. The sooner you attack the grease in the kitchen after cooking, the easier it will release its sticky grip.

Hanging things is an organizing technique that orderly people use often. They do it to keep surfaces clean, but it also helps when there are storage problems. Here are some quick hang-up tips for the kitchen:

The sooner you attack the grease in the kitchen after cooking, the easier it will release its sticky grip.

- Use hooks or an expandable accordion coatrack to hang up cups.
- Use hanging baskets for fruits and veggies. We had limes, avocados, and oranges that took up valuable counter space until I bought a hanging basket.
- Hang knives on a magnetic knife bar. It frees drawer space and keeps them from nicking and dulling each other in the drawer.
- Hang up brooms and mops. This gets them off the floor where they tend to fall over and clutter things, and it takes the pressure off the bristles, which could ruin them. You can buy holders for this purpose at the hardware store, or you can screw a metal eye into the top of the wooden handle and hang it on a cup hook mounted on the wall.

The backs of doors are very important for storage in the kitchen as well as other rooms. Put small wire shelves or racks for spices on the inside of cabinet doors. Racks that hold aluminum foil, bags, plastic wrap, soap, steel wool pads, and so on clear a lot of shelf space.

Cooking utensils can also be hung up, thus eliminating the clutter they cause in drawers. It is a good idea to hang measuring spoons on cup hooks inside a cabinet door. Hang pots on the wall, but be sure not to have so many things hanging on the walls in the kitchen that it begins to look cluttered. Since shelf and drawer space are at a premium in most homes, hang or stand up anything that can be hung or stood up.

Closely akin to hanging items is standing them up in containers. Both of these techniques work because vertical placement frees up the horizontal spaces of counter and drawer. In many cases they make the kitchen items more easily accessible.

A COOL WAY TO GO

The refrigerator is the most problematic area of the kitchen. If you have a neat little fridge that never gives you trouble, you will think the following ideas are excessive. But if you have spent time hungrily searching the refrigerator for a condiment, while hot food cools on the table, this approach will be a long-term blessing. Here is a place where the basic organizing approach really pays off.

First, group things together, all condiments, dressings, fruit, vegetables, meat—well, you get the idea. Designate different zones in the refrigerator for the various groups. You can do it by pulling everything out on the counter or just by rearranging it in the fridge.

Second, once you see clearly what you have in the refrigerator, simplify by getting rid of duplicates and things that have spoiled or have outlived their expiration date. Green, fuzzy stuff, dried-up food, food which is too old, and even "good" leftovers nobody wants need to be discarded quickly.

Finally, put the different groups of food into holders of various sorts. You will be surprised at how many appropriate baskets or boxes are available in stores today. You will discover square cornered containers are best. Because the refrigerator is so deep, the back of the box is often poorly used, harboring fugitive items for a long time. Your greatest difficulty will be finding containers that are deep enough to reach from the front to the

118

back of the refrigerator to make maximum use of space. When you look for something that is in the condiment container, say mustard, you pull the container out like a drawer and there it is!—readily available even if it was "way in the back." I write the names of what is in the jars on the lids so I can easily pick out sweet gherkins from dill chips when I look down into the container. Then I label the front of each container or "drawer" to identify the contents. For me, this is the Bare Bones Way. When the setup is complete, be sure to maintain it by returning the items where they belong in the proper container each time you use them.

You may think that this does not sound like the 80/20 rule of simplicity. But it is, because, once the system is set up, it will keep you from spending a lot of time looking for things in the refrigerator. After I set up my refrigerator into zones with labeled containers, my life became wonderfully simple.

Tips for the Kitchen

- Store items where they are used, such as dishes near the dishwasher and pots and pans near the stove.
- Keep pot lids in a pot lid holder. Some hang on the wall. Some people use a dish drainer in a cabinet to hold their pot lids.
- Use all of the room in your cabinet, not just the surface of the shelf. Three-tier wire racks expand storage of plates; the smaller plates stack above the larger ones on each tier. Hang cups from hooks under shelves.
- Peruse local stores and catalogs that sell kitchen organizing products. They will stimulate your thinking. But buy only what will meet your storage needs.
- Note leftovers *and* the date they were stored on a white board or on sticky notes on the refrigerator, so you can be aware of what is available.

119

- Store seldom used things high or in hard to reach spots. Buy a small one-step stool that you can keep handy to reach what is difficult to reach. Some of these little stools fold for easy storage.
- Keep the refrigerator at 38–40°F and the freezer at 0°F. To check the fridge temperature, place a thermometer designed to measure low temperatures in a glass of water and leave it in the middle of the refrigerator for eight hours. To check the freezer, place the thermometer between packages and check after eight hours. If need be, adjust the temperature controls and check again in five to eight hours. This is a time management tip, because if food spoils, you will lose a lot of time being sick.
- Download recipes off the Internet from sites such as FamilyCircle.com. Copy and paste favorites into a document or documents on your computer so you can find the wanted recipe easily by using the Find or Search button. This is so efficient, you will need to restrain yourself from collecting too many recipes. It clears shelves of cookbooks and card files, though most people will still want a standard cookbook and a few cards of favorites.
- Zone the cabinets by grouping canned and boxed goods. Put similar products like gravy mixes together into containers. Label the shelves and containers to remind yourself and the family where items are located.
- If you do nothing else, regularly use paper plates in place of those that need to be washed.

What Do You Really Want?

Look around your house and be specific as you answer these two questions.

What is your favorite part of the house?
Which part is the biggest problem?

Now take time to evaluate, on the scale below, all of the main rooms in the house to see which are most in need of improvement. Draw a scale like the one below to evaluate each room in your house. The storage areas will be considered later.

1	2	3	4	5
It is well organized				It needs a lot of organizing

Living area (including family room)   Bathroom(s) (list each)
Dining area   Children's rooms
Bedroom(s) (list each)   Guest bedroom
Others

The Bare Bones Way

As you have been reading about the various rooms, you have been deciding on the changes you want to make. Undoubtedly, there are many. The Bare Bones Way is to choose the ones that will make the biggest splash with the least effort.

Keeping in mind your brief evaluation above and the thoughts about your home that you've had, ask yourself, *If I had three wishes, and money, time, and energy were no concern, what would I change in my house?* This question will free you up to see what you really want but perhaps have not been admitting to yourself. You may already have an idea of what these three wishes are but you have not given them sufficient thought for ideas for change to crystallize.

To prime the pump further, walk around the house with a pencil and paper. Choose one thing in each room that you feel is a problem that needs to be solved. List that problem or in some cases problems. (Don't bother listing problems concerning paper control because that will be dealt with later.)

Now choose three of the problems you will focus on changing. If you feel frustrated in choosing only three in a sea of problems, remember that we are using the Bare Bones approach, choosing the top 20 percent that will make a significant difference.

Now set out to accomplish these three goals and only these three, one at a time. If you have not yet done the three Cs, get the white boxes recommended and do them now in the first area you have chosen. Just in case they have slipped your mind, the Cs are:

Consolidate. Group things together that are alike.

Containerize. Put them in drawers, boxes, baskets, and the like that are appropriate for the items.

Condense. Get rid of the things you don't want to put into the container once you see how many duplications, broken things, and excess you have.

Now tackle the first problem in the room you are working on. Perhaps it is a general storage problem. Do you need to rearrange the storage of items? Put things close to where they are used and are easy to access. How about rearranging the furniture? Do you need to get rid of something, perhaps a large piece of furniture? That's one thing that makes a big difference! Do you need to buy furniture so you will have more drawers or shelves for storage?

Don't bite off more than you can chew. Remember, we are streamlining our lives. If you solve just the few most significant problems, your life can be greatly improved.

After you care for the top three problems, choose three more if you wish. Keep going until the most crucial problems are solved. Ignore the smaller problems, the less important 80 percent, or do them later from time to time as you continue to maintain the house.

The projects you have decided to focus on are where you will place your time and attention. The toughest problem will melt in the heat of sustained focus.

The toughest problem will melt in the heat of sustained focus.

Decision Time—Choose Your Top 20 Percent

My first three primary goals in the order they will be tackled are:

1.
2.
3.

The next three:

1.
2.
3.

Of course, there will be others that will follow in the future, but the likelihood is that caring for six organizing projects will make a huge difference. Using the mathematics of Prieto's 80/20 principle, three projects represent the most important of fifteen organizing improvements that could be done around the house and six represents the most important of thirty. To put it another way, these three to six projects will make a whale of a difference in your house.

8
∎

You Can Clean Your House in Fifteen Minutes a Day—or Maybe Thirty on a Bad Day

It's Not Brain Surgery—Just Do It

Cleaning is just one of those mundane but inescapable facts of life. Without clean surroundings we feel poorly about ourselves and apologetic when company comes.

Like other tasks that aren't high on our favorites list, it's much easier if broken into smaller pieces. Making it easy to do quick spot cleaning as part of your regular routines keeps things from building into big, discouraging jobs.

Keep your tools and supplies easily reachable for each area. For example, make a cleaning kit for each bathroom and the kitchen. A small tote holds a multipurpose spray cleaner, toilet cleaner (for bathroom), brushes, and cloths. Mount a paper towel holder near each sink or inside a cabinet door and do a quick clean of the counters, sink and mirrors often.

Decluttering always makes it easier to clean. Organize hair, cosmetic, and other supplies into containers. Then you can just move the container to clean.

Routine decluttering and quick cleanups make life easier. Simplified cleaning is the way to go.

Leslie Robison
Simple Systems Organizing
Green Lane, Pennsylvania
www.cluttersmith.com

At first, we just want to get the floor clean and be able to eat on the dining room table without having to clear it off. We just want to get rid of the clutter. But somewhere down the line, as we improve, we begin to yearn for shining surfaces. When we begin to see the floor, the top of the table, and anything else that will take a shine, we begin to dream of gleaming surfaces.

Shining tabletops, floors, counters, even sinks can be inspiration for our souls. From those shining spots, we draw strength to keep going till we have more and more of those shining surfaces in our homes. Maybe, after a while, the whole house will take on a glow.

What Do You Want?

On which end of the continuum are your desires?

1	2	3	4	5
I don't care much about how clean the house looks.			The house must be perfect at all times.	

1	2	3	4	5
I'm happy if the dust is not overly obvious.			I want shining surfaces everywhere.	

125

1	2	3	4	5
I want floors you can eat off, because there is plenty of food down there.				I want spotless floors at all times.

1	2	3	4	5
I'm happy with a kitchen sink with only a few dirty dishes.				My sink must be empty and sparkling.

1	2	3	4	5
Food rules can be casual.				No food or drink in the living room or bedrooms.

1	2	3	4	5
I like a lived-in look.			I like a model home look.	

The Bare Bones Way

Annalbert (I kid you not—that was her name—a family thing, I guess) and I were standing side by side in the coffee emporium pouring sweet powder from little pink packets into our coffee cups. I was piling my empty packets on the counter, planning to throw them away when I finished. Annalbert never let her packets touch the counter. They were dropped directly into the trash receptacle.

Something about her movements rang a bell in my head. She was efficiently skipping a step in cleaning! *Here is a naturally organized person,* I thought! So I introduced myself and conducted a short interview. She told me what I suspected she would tell me.

"I work full-time," she said, "and I have a two-year-old at home. That makes a difference in how I clean my house. I am not compulsive"—she waved her hand as if to dismiss that idea—"but I am an organized person. I like to keep things nice."

"How much time do you spend a week cleaning house?" I asked.

Thinking briefly she told me she spent about four hours on weekends actually cleaning. (In my opinion that is a long time for sustained cleaning, especially on a regular basis.) During the week she had to cook for her husband and take care of her child when she got home from work, so she didn't have time to clean then. Even as she cleaned on the weekend, her child was underfoot. She looked at her feet and wiggled her fingers like a child scurrying about.

"The secret is keeping things up all during the week, not letting them get out of control. I maintain the house all the time."

I thanked Annalbert, who told me I could use her name and made sure I knew it was pronounced Ann-albert, not Annal-bert as we parted.

Annalbert has her method. It is a variation of the Bare Bones method because it is simple and streamlined. It works for her and it confirms that no matter how you spread out your cleaning, you don't need to spend large amounts of time.

IN THE TRENCHES WITH SMART HOMEMAKERS

From Janet:

Set a timer and do 10 minutes only—*then* reward yourself. The reward is essential—watch 10 minutes of TV, have an ice cream, just something small, but a reward that you know you have deserved and can repeat when later on you do another 10 minutes and have your reward. The reason for the rewards is to engender within you that a little bit of cleaning up often is a good thing, and there is a reward for doing so. Eventually the reward comes from doing the task itself—but that can be a way off yet.

Eventually you will have a little piece of paradise in your house. Make an announcement that this is *your* space, and *no one*, and I mean *no one* has the right to mess it up or put anything there that does not belong. This is your reminder that one day your house will be tidy too.

Then give yourself some time to make it first priority to keep this place clean. Not a big task every day or you will be discouraged that keeping clean is too much. Just a little bit often will keep the paradise.

When you have achieved this, you do the adjoining piece or another piece. Step-by-step you make little restful places in your house. When the mess gets you down, you go and look at this place, and it will calm you down—or motivate you to do some more.

This was a really important step for me when I began to clean up—and when I need some motivation to keep doing it, this is how I get going again.

Variations on the Cleaning Theme

I asked Betty and Susie, who work in my dentist's office, about their cleaning habits. You need to know that both are from backgrounds that have a cultural bent toward very fastidious housecleaning, so their time is spent maintaining a very high level of tidiness. The Bare Bones method applies because both of them do their work efficiently, using a minimum of time for the level they want to maintain.

Betty spreads a little cleaning over the days of the week. Recently divorced, she lives with her fourteen-year-old daughter and eleven-year-old son. Her floor is white tile, which she sweeps and mops daily before she goes to work. It takes thirty to forty minutes each morning but is important to her because she doesn't want to come home to a "dirty" house. Her one complaint is that, although her children are tidy and keep things picked up, her daughter never makes her bed, so Betty does it for her. She has very high standards and spends about four hours cleaning on the weekend.

Her one confession of failure is that she does not schedule time for filing receipts and they pile up.

Her coworker Susie, wife and working mother of two young children, hung her head and giggled. "Oh, you are going to think I am a pig," she said. "I spend only fifteen or twenty minutes a day on the house, sometimes not that."

"Do you schedule time to clean?"

"Oh no! I do it when I see it needs to be done! If you came to my house, you would find it all looks fine. Mainly I clean while I'm doing other things. If I see the tub needs cleaning when I am showering, I just do it then."

She told how she does dishes by hand because it is so little to do that it is easier than using her dishwasher. (Has the woman lost her mind? My dishwasher is my most beloved appliance!) Then, because her mother did it, she stores the clean dishes and silverware in the refrigerator and the cups in the freezer "for ice cream and things." I told her she had been reading too many medical books on germs.

When I asked her if she scheduled chores for certain times, she said, "That's not the real world. Who has time for that?"

As she thought about it, she concluded that since things were going so well she guessed there was no need to make a change. And for her, there is no need. She is definitely a high maintainer, a Bare Bones cleaner.

Seek the level that is right for you, whether high or not so high. But when you determine the level you want, don't plan to spend your hours cleaning if a more condensed method can do it in minutes.

Cleaning with a Q-Tip?

Because I am an organizer, people like to talk to me about how they clean their houses. "Do you know what my favorite cleaning instrument is?" someone asked. When I said I didn't, she told me, "It's a Q-Tip! I just love to clean in little spots with my Q-Tips." She wiggled an imaginary one as this enthusiastic detailer explained the joy of cleaning.

I think we can safely say that, with rare exception, cleaning with Q-Tips is not a regular part of the Bare Bones cleaning plan.

Only two kinds of people are superfastidious about cleaning—those who are very organized and clean, like my friend with the Q-Tip, and those who are very disorganized. We understand the first easily enough. The second group, however, requires some explanation.

Disorganized people may be fastidious cleaners in a special way. Sometimes they substitute cleaning the sink, oven, toilet, or some specific spot perfectly for cleaning the whole house. Of course, focusing on and controlling one spot does not address the problem if the rest of the house remains messy. This is not the Bare Bones Way.

On the other hand, sometimes conquering a significant spot can activate the CAN DO! attitude that can springboard you toward improving the whole house. If used in that way, it can be helpful.

Good Enough Is Good Enough

Organizing and cleaning are kissing cousins. When you are striving to organize your house, somewhere along the way comes the urge to clean things up a bit more, to put a shine on the faucet and a gleam on the lamp table. This is understandable and laudable. Just be sure you are cleaning at a level that is comfortable for you to maintain.

In the Bare Bones spirit, we look for the 20 percent that will make the 80 percent difference. What is that

20 percent? Let's step back and look dispassionately at the cleaning process.

SIMPLIFY YOUR PRODUCTS

Focusing on limited but excellent cleaning is a waste of time and energy. It is like a well, deep but narrow. The Bare Bones Way is like a river, broad but shallow. And that is the way cleaning works best in modern society.

The days of working one's fingers to the bone for a sparkling clean house have pretty much faded away. The white-glove-test standard got started when modern cleaning appliances became available to already hard-working stay-at-home women. The combination of old work habits with new technology kicked housekeeping into warp speed. Women vied with each other to have the cleanest laundry hanging on the line early Monday morning (with undies hidden behind or in pillowcases for modesty's sake). They chased dirt and dust from every corner. It was a truly tidy time.

But things have changed. Today people who do cleaning for a hobby may indulge themselves if they get a kick out of it, but the rest of us just want to do a good job with less effort. We have pretty much stepped away from the whole illusion of fastidious detailing.

THE SIMPLE WAY

Naturally organized cleaners use a plan we can copy. Following their streamlined example, you need to choose only a few products you have found work for you—a glass cleaner, a few kitchen and bathroom cleaners, toilet bowl cleaner, and one or two items that meet the specialty needs in your house. Avoid adding new products that promise to do more, smell better, or offer some other advantage but are really just duplicates of what you already have. Those who read books on cleaning tips even buy mineral spirits, turpentine, vinegar, dry

In addition to simplifying your cleaning products, simplify your house. Don't introduce hard-to-clean surfaces into your life.

washing soda, denatured alcohol, and other products at the hardware store for specialty cleaning problems, which only call for more effort. While intriguing, using so many products complicates the whole process.

Decide which products you want, and don't switch until the products you now have are gone and if the change is for a good reason. That way you won't accumulate half-used bottles of cleaner.

In addition to simplifying your cleaning products, simplify your house. Don't introduce hard-to-clean surfaces into your life. Trying to clean white rugs, hard-to-maintain kitchen counters, wicker or cane tables, chandeliers or complex hanging lighting, tufted upholstery, and the like is asking for trouble. When buying items for your home, choose those that are simple to maintain. This is the Bare Bones Way.

The Fifteen-Minute Plan—or Maybe Thirty

As mentioned in the chapter on maintenance, you will find a marvelous change if you dedicate only fifteen (or perhaps thirty) minutes a day to the house. Many people report the magic of the fifteen-minute plan. They set their kitchen timer or put on music that lasts about that long. Day by day they zip around for fifteen minutes doing their cleaning thing. You can name it the Fifteen-Minute Frenzy if you move fast enough. If your house is very large or has some special needs, you may want to do an extra fifteen minutes either added to the first fifteen minutes or later in the day. The truth is that once you get started, you will probably overshoot the fifteen minutes on a reasonably consistent basis. But remember, you don't have to. You only commit for fifteen minutes at a time.

If you should find that the Fifteen-Minute Frenzy does not do the trick for you, consider adding an additional Ten-Minute Tidy. (This name comes from a children's television program, but it works for adults as well.) Throw that in during another part of the day. Of course, some special situations may take longer, but we are aiming to maintain a clean house in a few, short, habitual periods of time.

After routinely using this method, the house will probably become good enough to have drop-in company, to have family and friends as houseguests, or most important of all, to enjoy it yourself without feeling that you should be up and doing something around the house.

You will be amazed at what you can accomplish with consistent movement, no matter how small, in the right direction. The motto of The-Organizer-Lady Yahoo! group is "The secret to success is making very small, yet very consistent, changes." If you try to change too quickly, you will scare yourself and be tempted to turn back to your old way of life. Someone coined the saying, "Never underestimate the inevitability of gradualness." Others who remember the movie *What about Bob?* say it more simply as Bob's long-suffering psychologist did with the words, "Baby steps, baby steps!"

Whatever way you say it, the truth is that you don't have to engage in marathon and Herculean cleaning projects. Just move consistently and mindfully in the right direction.

A little dab will do you. That is the Bare Bones Way.

WHERE TO SPEND YOUR FIFTEEN MINUTES

Okay, so you've got your fifteen-minute commitment set up—and maybe ten minutes more to boot where necessary. But where in the house will you invest those minutes? The house has three kinds of areas—the public areas, the private or family areas, and storage areas. Without a plan, you will be doubling back on work already done and neglecting areas that need attention.

The best idea is to find a simple plan that spreads out the cleaning plan over the days of the week.

- Some do it by zones, designating a room or area a day.
- Others organize by listing tasks like vacuum the house, clean bathroom fixtures, or dust the furniture, and do what they can in fifteen minutes. The value of doing jobs that are alike is that once you have your supplies out, you can use them to the maximum.
- Some go from large items—here we include picking up clutter—to smaller items, such as putting away dishes, to dust and dirt, which is loose, and finally to washing what has jelled into grime.

Others get real complicated with their plan, schedule each job, and take it all very seriously. This is not our approach. That is beyond the Bare Bones Way.

Keep it really simple. Remember that we are aiming for finding the golden 20 percent that makes an impact.

Maybe scheduling only fifteen minutes seems crazy. There *are* problems to consider and solve. The cleaning plan won't be effective if you or your family is dirtying up faster than cleaning up. There are certain contributing factors to think about if the Bare Bones method is going to work.

First and foremost, your family has got to be a part of the solution, not part of the problem. The ideal thing is for them to join in the Fifteen-Minute Frenzy, either in their own rooms or in some area you designate for them to clean.

The house has got to be reasonably well organized, as suggested earlier in the book, for this fifteen-minute plan to move forward successfully. You and your family have got to be working the five habits of order maintenance (see chap. 2) as a regular part of organizational life, so the house will look reasonably neat. Something is not quite right if you try to keep your house clean while it is cluttered. A vacuumed rug with stuff piled on it, or even one sock in the middle, doesn't bring about the effect you desire.

> Something is not quite right if you try to keep your house clean while it is cluttered.

Cleaning makes sense only if you have a house that is easy to work in, at least the parts you and others see. You need to have the house look neat for your own sake. The truth is that it is very difficult to work up motivation to clean (as in vacuum and dust) a cluttered house.

Some will say they clean for health reasons, but that is a secondary motivation and is not inspiring. Health is important, but the primary motivation for anything we do in the house is aesthetic. Cleaning enhances the basic good look of the house into which you have already built beauty by organizing and decorating. You want your heart to leap with joy when you walk into your beautiful, and now clean, house.

WHAT DO I DO FIRST?

Don Aslett wrote the book *Do I Dust or Vacuum First?*[1] The question reflects the problem of deciding what order to use in cleaning. The logical pattern for cleaning is twofold: top to bottom and in to out.

Top to bottom implies that in the house you start from the upper floor and work down to the lower floor. That may be all in one day (I faint just thinking about it!) or over several days' time. In an individual room, it means dusting or cleaning what is higher and working down until you get to the floor.

Cleaning from *in to out* implies that you clean the closets, drawers, cabinets, and the like first. Then you work from the walls outward into the middle of the room.

Although the logic of this is indisputable, there are obviously some cases in which special areas will require a change in the pattern. Some people will not like this pattern. They will have their own pattern or work randomly without much of a pattern. They just follow an item-by-item or area-by-area approach (preferably written down so nothing is missed) without attention to *in and out* or *up to down*.

Any of these will probably work. The best approach is one that will get the maximum done on the most regular basis whether it makes sense or not. Just do your fifteen minutes faithfully one way or the other. A crazily organized fifteen minutes will probably accomplish nearly as much as a well-organized time.

IN THE TRENCHES WITH SMART HOMEMAKERS

From Loni:

I have had numerous "systems." I tried cleaning one room a day. You'd think this would work, but it didn't. I also tried vacuuming on Mondays, dusting on Tuesdays, etc., but this didn't last long either. Lately, I've made a list of chores that need to be done daily, such as making the bed, wiping out microwave, kitchen counter, stove, etc. These are things that if neglected, the house will appear dirty. Each night I check off the items I've accomplished. This seems to work very well except on the days that I have a lot of outside activities. Today, nothing was accomplished. I don't have a paying job anymore, but I have several volunteer jobs, and I spend a lot of time on the phone (and computer).

THE OUNCE OF PREVENTION THING

The best kind of cleaning is that which does not have to be done because you are careful not to let the house get dirty. This does not mean constant yelling at folks to be more careful. It means setting up the house and habits so dirt doesn't happen. Well, not so much anyway.

Rugs long enough to catch shoe debris at the entrances of the house will do wonders in keeping the floor clean. It is best to be able to take several steps forward on the entrance rugs as in banks and other public buildings. Those rugs aren't there for aesthetics. They are part of the preventive cleaning plan.

Watch out for making messes you will have to come back and clean up. Put down paper to catch peelings when cooking. Keep books and knickknacks behind glass on shelves so they won't need dusting so much. Transfer liquid over a sink in case it spills. Have a large garbage bag available for papers and ribbon when opening presents. Put tops over spattering foods on the stove and don't let cooking food overflow. Use deep enough dishes when cooking in the oven so food won't spill over. Put stirring spoons on a special holder not on the stove top or counter.

You get the idea. Be alert. Think ahead. Some things we can't avoid, such as skin cells falling off our bodies onto the furniture. Don't laugh. About 40 percent of the "dust" we see is really skin cells. But we do what is within our power to stay tidy and then we clean up the rest as quickly and easily as possible.

POWER HOUR

Carla, homeschooler of two teens and mother of a preschooler, has back problems. Well, it is really more complicated than that, but we won't go there. Tom, her husband, instituted an hour on Saturday that he calls the Power Hour. During that time, the family, especially he and the older children, devote an hour to heavier chores that need to be done. Three hard workers can get a whale of a lot of work done in an hour's time.

The Power Hour is a good idea for those heavy jobs that don't get caught up in the short time blocks during the week.

Beyond Bare Bones

Doing things the simple way all the time is not for everybody. One morning you wake up with added vigor. Spring is in the air. You are able to open the windows and cool breezes stir your blood. Your hormones are at the most creative point of the month, or perhaps you feel the nesting urge because a new little one is on the way. In short, you *want* to overdo. You feel it is your calling! Your heritage! You want to redecorate. You may even feel the desire to (gasp!) remodel.

When the urge to go over the top comes, there are many books that will guide you into the stratosphere of cleanliness. Don Aslett has written many books on cleaning as have Jeff Campbell and his Clean Team. For more information on cleaning than anyone could ever want or use, obtain the encyclopedic volume *Home Comforts*.[2] New books come out regularly. Peruse your local bookstore and library for inspiring tomes. Large online bookstores can easily guide you to their household cleaning section of books.

Some people feel more comfortable when their lives are carefully structured. They love schedules. For them it is desirable to have a master list in which the household maintenance is neatly nailed down.

During the month, there is a designated day for:

- car care
- filing and purging files
- cleaning and purging thc rcfrigerator
- clothes closet cleaning
- linen closet straightening
- purse cleaning and purging

During the year there are various days designated on the calendar for jobs such as:

- attic maintenance
- garage cleaning
- basement attention

People who enjoy having schedules to remind them and keep them on track may even include gutter cleaning, gardening reminders, window attention, changing air conditioner filters, and the like.

Bare Bones Tips

The Bare Bones Way is different. Here are some tips:

- If you live in a wet, muddy, or snowy area, make a spot at the door for removal of boots, hanging mittens, and the like. Provide a place to sit to inspire family members to take care of muddy shoes and drippy clothes.
- Set up and label a WHATZIT BOX. Strange things of unknown origin show up from time to time in the house. A metal nut, some plastic piece, a stray glove, or piece of toy go into the box for possible future retrieval.
- Hate cleaning but love cleaning products? This is common. Wanting to change products for the sake of novelty and

hope for better results keeps us jumping from product to product, often leaving half-used, abandoned products languishing in the cabinet, causing clutter. Finish up or throw away one cleaning product before buying another brand of the same type.

- Cleaning is a boring job for many people. Choose to clean listening to a continuing story tape or CD while you work. The lure of the story will bring you back to the job each day and the fun of the story will make you enjoy the whole process more.

- As much as possible, clean windows by using extensions that attach to your hose. Eventually, you will need to follow the classic hands-on method to get the inside done and give special attention to screens. Because it is such a big job, gather helpers to wash windows with you or hire workers to do it for you. If none of this is possible, wait for the right weather and then do it a little at a time—possibly one room a day. Don Aslett's book *Is There Life after Housework?*[3] detailed about how to use a squeegee to make cleaning windows easier.

Beyond Bare Bones Tips

- Put lettuce in a clean pillowcase into the washer spin cycle to dry it for salad. (I didn't make this one up, I swear.)
- Have guests remove shoes when entering the house.
- Dust the fuse box.
- Spray newly polished white shoes with hair spray to keep the white from smearing.
- Whiten socks by boiling them in water to which a slice of lemon has been added. I, for one, would hesitate to use that pot later for cooking.
- Cover the top of the refrigerator with clear plastic wrap. When it is dirty, simply peel it off.

All of these are pretty good ideas but very far away from Bare Bones basics. However, remember, any tip, no matter how useless it may seem, is a good tip if it solves a chronic problem, which has been making you do more work. For example, putting adhesive tape on the bottom of rockers that keep scratching your newly polished wooden floor is a great idea if you have this problem.

Decision Time—Choose Your Top 20 Percent

Here are three changes in or additions to my cleaning plan that will help me focus on what is important and keep the house clean with the least effort:

1.
2.
3.

9

The Fam—Friend or Foe

Cupboard Cubbies

When our children were growing up, I found a great way to keep the kitchen countertops from becoming a dumping ground. I decided to clear out one cupboard per child in the kitchen where I could stash their stuff. Over the years they could be found squatting at their cupboard sorting, stuffing, or cleaning it out. If I found something lying on the counters that belonged to one of the kids I would open their cupboard and pop it inside—out of my sight and off my mind! Tears still come to my eyes when I recall my daughter's wedding day. I can still picture her sitting on the kitchen floor in front of her cupboard for the last time. She has three children of her own now. I wonder when they'll get their cupboards? Maybe I should make one for each of them at grandma's house!

Judy Warmington
Woman Time Management
Hudsonville, Michigan
www.womantimemanagement.com

The Tendency to Overdo

Now more than ever before, moms and dads are working themselves to death helping the kids work themselves to death with clubs, classes, teams, church activities, school activities, and extracurricular school activities. For many it is a modern lifestyle choice. Many parents feel they should give their children opportunities in many different areas, that they should help create memories that their children will carry for a lifetime.

Families with several children are hard-pressed to coordinate their schedules. Because of working schedules and safety factors, adult-supervised activities are becoming more common. In many areas, neighborhood life has changed. Few kids are home in the afternoon, so supervised and structured activities outside the home are becoming the norm.

When parents and young children spend time sitting through sports activities of older children, waiting for their classes to finish, and traveling back and forth, they are experiencing an away-from-home lifestyle that begins to be hard on everyone. When activities multiply and younger children can't be left home alone, they are overstressed and fatigued from traveling around with a parent, depositing and waiting for the older children. The family van becomes a moving but inadequate family room. Time, which in the past was spent face to face in personal contact, is now spent hip to hip, facing forward in the car, at games, or at other activities.

Not that all of this is bad. Often, the children are benefiting. But the question is whether the frenetic schedule is too high a price for the benefit. The children are building memories. They become accustomed to and learn to love the stimulation, but some parents, looking back on their own more tranquil childhoods, wonder if the memories of their children will be meaningful ones.

Fatigue and Time Pressure

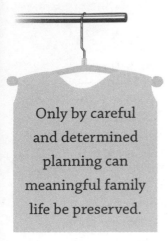

Only by careful and determined planning can meaningful family life be preserved.

The basic question in families is how they will use the time they have been allotted. Dr. James Dobson, psychologist and founder of Focus on the Family, states, "Time pressure will tear a family apart quicker than anything else."[1]

Speaking of the one factor that has done more damage to families than any other, Mark Twain stated that scheduling too much was "the almost universal condition of fatigue and time pressure, which leaves every member of the family exhausted and harried. Many of them have nothing left to invest in their marriages or in the nurturing of children."

Fatigue and time pressure—if it was a problem in Mark Twain's day, what is it in ours? Let us bring balance to our lives so that we can invest in what is important. Like a tornado, modern life slings family members in different directions from the core of the home. Once started, it is difficult to slow down. Only by careful and determined planning can meaningful family life be preserved.

To increase quality time, pare down extraneous activities to a minimum and engage in family activities to the maximum. Use the house as a good clean canvas on which to paint the value and pleasures of family life.

If your present way of life relies on a crowded calendar, perhaps even color coded, to keep you on schedule, perhaps you need to consider whether there are activities that could be jettisoned from your life. Do the hard job of picking the top 20 percent that give 80 percent of the satisfaction, and eliminate the rest.

Slowing Down

Slowing down is just what many families are doing. More and more parents are questioning this full-steam-ahead way of life. After trying to have it all, many are waking up to the unreality of that goal. Choices need to be made, peripherals need to be let go, and activities that reflect core values must be embraced more tightly.

There seems to be something of a trend toward the value of family time, tradition, comfort, and sacrifice of individuals for others in the family. Businesses are becoming more flexible, providing time for special family activities. Mothers and fathers who would not previously have taken off time for children's activities (or if they did kept it quiet) now do so openly and perhaps proudly. Stay-at-home moms, and even stay-at-home dads, say with their actions how much they value their place in raising their children. And though I know of no survey on the topic, I suspect more desks in the world of commerce, which were formerly devoid of any distraction from the business at hand, now display family photos.

Home Becomes More Important

Sometimes parents schedule outside activities because they are fearful that if their children stay home, they will waste time watching television or playing electronic games. To avoid this, parents need to declare technology-free hours. With no technology and no scheduled activities, won't children become bored if they have no diversions? Actually, boredom, rightly used, is very beneficial. It forces children to tap into their creative juices and develop their inner lives. When C. S. Lewis was bored as a child, he created an imaginary world, which later surfaced in the Chronicles of Narnia.

It is not easy to make the change and slow down. During the transition to more home-based activities, parents need to provide suggestions, props, games, building or art supplies, sports equipment, or whatever it takes to ease the child into imagination and creativity.

As the value of the family ascends, so does the importance of having a nice home and of working together as a team in the home. "Housework" is not something unpleasant Mom does and tries to rope the kids into when she can. It is the whole family working together toward a mutual goal of preparing a place of comfort and harmony "for the betterment of all who dwell therein."

What Do You Want?

Dream a little. If you had that magic wand so often spoken of when people are wishing for more in life, what would your wish be for your family? The possibilities are so broad. What are the first three things that come to mind that you would like for your family if changes were easily made with no effort on your part?

The Bare Bones Way

Depressurizing schedules is the basis of the Bare Bones process, but it is not the whole story. What moms, and dads to some extent, want is more prosaic and practical. They really want cooperative kids who will keep their rooms neat and help with household chores in a responsible way. If kids were to do those two things, most parents would be delighted.

This does not happen automatically. The dynamics of getting the family to help isn't complicated, but for some moms, applying simple organizing rules is not easy.

These first two postings from the trenches express how many moms feel from time to time.

IN THE TRENCHES WITH SMART HOMEMAKERS

From Susan:

I am overwhelmed! Never realized it was so overwhelming until I sat back and listened to Focus on the Family radio program this morning, and today I am staying home from a Moms in Touch rally that I have been looking forward to because once again the house is too messy for a good mom to leave it like this to face "after school" and a busy weekend. Ugghhhh . . . here we go again . . .

From a Mom of Seven:

I am a 41 yo homemaker with 7 children. Fortunately I don't homeschool and currently I only have my 2 youngest home with me all day.

Keeping up with 7 kids and a 2400 sq. ft house is overwhelming, especially when I'm the only one picking up and cleaning. If it gets too far gone, my husband helps.

I've tried all the lists, the chore charts, taking their things, grounding them, etc., and nothing has motivated my family so far to help me. Some of them have even gone so far as to remove cleaning instructions from the walls where I have posted them. If I ever figure who did that, someone will be in big trouble.

I need help in "organizing" my life and my home so that I'm not mortified when someone pulls up in my driveway or when my kids want to have company (which by the way I do not allow because their rooms are always a wreck and they just don't care).

It's up to Mom to step in to move things in the right direction. What does it take to move from being overwhelmed to being in control? Just applying rules? It is not as simple as it seems because the secret is first of all attitude and secondly the will to take control. Only after these are in place, do the rules become important.

These moms have decided to train their families to be responsible.

From a Stay-At-Home Mom:

I decided I am not responsible for every little thing in the house, just because I'm the stay-at-home mom. So, every one has chores, even 4 yr. old. She swiffs (mops with a Swiffer), puts laundry into the front-loading washer, and puts her clothes away from the dry clothesbasket. If you have several children and a husband, you shouldn't have to do anything but cook, maybe vacuum the main rooms, and oversee everything else. You don't have to do it all! So what if the vacuuming they do isn't perfect? You didn't have to do it. So what if the dusting missed a little spot one week? They'll catch it next time. Children can properly do anything you inspect and expect. My little one keeps her underwear sorted in baskets she can reach—it took me weeks to get her trained, but I no longer do it for her. I don't put my husband's underwear away either—that's his job.

On the Toy Patrol:

One thing that really helped me was to go thru all the toys and get rid of most of them! I got rid of all the toys that they just picked up, looked at, and dropped. I only kept the educational toys and books and the toys that had multipurpose ways to play with them, like Tinker toys, Duplos, blocks, train set, Lincoln logs, car rug, and cars, etc. Just the creative ones. We also have the rule that they can play with only one thing at a time, unless they're playing with 2 things together. So they have to pick up the toy they're finished with *before they go on to anything else.* No snack, etc. unless they pick it up. Otherwise they get sidetracked and I'd forget about it in another room and then they'd be another mess out someplace else! It takes some time bending over them at first, making sure everything gets picked up, but then they get in the habit of it.

"Rules" That Work:

I wash clothes that are *in* the hamper.
Everyone puts away *their* clothes from the basket.

148

Everyone carries their own dishes to the kitchen after eating.

Put away what you get out when you are through with it (when you go to bed, you're through! This requires having a home for everything & dumping things with no home.)

No snacks in bedrooms.

No sticky drinks in the car.

Do it now. (This refers to spills. Clean them before they get tracked all over.)

Plan for as much as possible, but don't be too busy to play.

I never thought I'd have routines or rules like my Cleanie mother, but it certainly has helped. I don't panic anymore when people are about to drop by (which is good since our house is on the market). The odd thing is, I have just as much time for sewing as I did when we spent 30 minutes every day looking for lost things!

From Jennifer:
Well, we have been playing "decently and in order" while cleaning the living room for about 21 days now. I think I need to play it a little longer, though the girls get excited when we clean it that way because it seems soooo much easier.

We were able to do the dining room, kitchen, living room, hall, and entry in 45 minutes. That included vacuuming and mopping. (And not one argument from them about the tasks—maybe aliens took them over.)

Making It a Game:
I decided to play this game with all the kids. My 4 year old is the only one who really understood, but that was okay. I set the timer (oven timer) for 5 min. and said we had to pick everything up off the living room floor before the timer went off. After 5 minutes were over and we had raced around trying to hurry before the timer went off, we had made so much progress and she enjoyed it so much, we decided to set it for another 3. By this point most of the room was picked up and I was able to vacuum.

149

Kids' Memorabilia:
What about your kids' trophies from all of their sporting events? I hate the thought of throwing them out, but the kids are older now (21 and 18), and they don't want them. One thing I will suggest to those of you with younger kids. Whenever your kids come home with a project or paper they are proud of, take a picture of them holding it. Even a trophy. Had I done this all along, I wouldn't be having this dilemma of what to do with all of this childhood stuff. I'm so bad, I have teeth, hair, shoes, etc. but don't know what belonged to who . . . sigh.

Your Family Can Help

Teach your kids and husband how to help out! Be honest. Is there a perfectionist in you that won't allow anyone else to do something if the results are less than perfect? Do you keep doing certain chores because you think you're the only one who knows how to do them right? Well, think back. How do you learn to do things? How many mistakes did you make? Let go and let your family learn, not just from your example but by trying things themselves. Kids can do laundry and help with cooking, cleaning, and yard work. It teaches them not only how to actually accomplish certain tasks but also that families are teams and need to work together. It allows them to contribute to the team effort. It has never hurt anyone to discover that there is no housekeeping fairy who magically sees that it all gets done. Your kids' future mates will be grateful. And aren't there times that you wish someone had taught your husband that having someone to pick up after him is not his God-given right?

Spotlight on Hubby

The marriage counselor asked Sharon what it would take to make her realize that Jake really loved her. How

would she like him to express his love to her? She replied that, as much as she appreciated flowers and kind words he brought to her office with a flourish, what she really wanted was for him to take the initiative in doing the routine, necessary jobs around the house. She worked a full-time job as did he. She was just as tired as he was. She needed part of his time and energy so that she would have more of her own. Compared to that gift, flowers, candy, and the like came off as penny-ante stuff in her view.

Let go and let your family learn, not just from your example but by trying things themselves.

Most men don't realize how much women need and want support in the home, not only for practical reasons but as an expression of caring. A recent study indicates that women are more amorous with husbands who do inside housework because it telegraphs "I love you" in a genuine way.

Maybe Jake substituted the traditional flower expressions of love for the meaningful work expression that costs him more than a bunch of flowers (welcomed as they might be from time to time). Or perhaps he is pretty disorganized himself and doesn't know how to help. Or possibly Sharon needs to communicate with him what she needs in a way that makes sense to him As she discovered later, Jake resented being told what to do no matter how sweetly expressed, but he loved written lists and would vigorously go about doing *anything* to happily cross those jobs off his list.

Whenever two people work together on one project, various complications need to be addressed and worked out to the benefit of both. That is particularly true when the project is a day-to-day, shoulder-to-shoulder activity, such as maintaining the house.

There are two ways the house relates to the family: The house supports the family, and the family supports the house.

The House Supports the Family

The house plays an important part in the life of the family as a whole and of the individual family members. To do its job well, the house must look good and work well.

When you as an adult walk into the house away from the troublesome world outside, you need the comfort of an environment that visually supports your spirit. You need a place to which you are proud to invite friends. You want a place that works well for you, where you can find things easily and do jobs efficiently.

Little kids want to be able to have friends over to play. Although it is not well developed, on some level children make judgments about how nice a house is. In their innocence, a young one who visits may say, "This house is messy."

Teens are sensitive to everything in their lives, including the condition of the house. They want a teen-friendly house into which they can invite their friends. Many alert parents even want to lure their child's friends into a teen-friendly house so they can get to know their child's all-important peers.

The Family Supports the House

Having no strength or will of its own, the house relies on the family to take care of it properly. Principles on how to do this is what this book is all about. Read my book *Neat Moms, Messie Kids*[2] for special ideas on how to rally the fam to work together as a team in keeping the house in order and running well.

The key principle here is that those who benefit from the house (insert here the names of all of your family members) are a part of the maintenance of how it works and looks. Too many family systems throw the weight of the house entirely on the back of the "woman of the house." While it is true she may be the manager, coach, owner, or however you want to put it, of the team, she is not the team and she certainly can't play all the positions. In some households it even begins to look like the mom is the clean team and the family members are the opposition dirty team.

Nothing could be further from the truth. The family team ought to work together to win. Winning is defined by having a house that looks good and works well with minimal effort (the Bare Bones Way) on the part of everyone. If, in their immaturity, family members don't appreciate the value or importance of a well-kept house, it is the job of the coach (that's you!) to inspire them.

Tips for the Fam

- Communicate information to family members. Two communication devices—the yearlong calendar and a whiteboard—are superimportant for even the smallest family. They are absolutely vital for larger ones. Use a yearlong calendar, preferably one of the large ones about 3 × 4 feet, which can be found in office supply stores. Mount it on a wall or door within easy view of the family but out of the public areas. Record any appointment or activity on the calendar. Include any pertinent information, such as address or phone number, beside the recording. Use the information on your calendar to keep the lid on overdoing.

  Place a whiteboard for recording needed supplies with an erasable pen placed in a convenient spot, perhaps on the refrigerator. Many like to include a corkboard and thumbtacks or magnets on the refrigerator to hold important coupons, invitations, and such.

- Use a toy box? As mentioned earlier, try to avoid big toy boxes altogether. They are alright when limited to storing large toys, such as big stuffed animals or large trucks. But disaster happens because children (and sometimes parents) find it convenient to clean up quickly by tossing everything, including Legos, small plastic farm animals, puzzle pieces, doll clothes, and little bits and pieces of toys, into the toy box. Pretty soon toys turn into debris in the bottom of the box. New toys are bought to replace the "lost" ones and, if the pattern is allowed to continue, the new ones will join the march to the bottom of the toy box.
- Train the children. Take time to train, carefully train, the children to do various jobs, such as setting the table, making their bed, doing laundry, mopping the floor. Make a list of steps they must learn for each job. Certify them when they are fully trained by giving them a certificate of accomplishment duly dated and signed. You can keep these in a special notebook.
- Manage toys. Any toy that is found where it does not belong should be put in "jail." To bail it out, the child must do a significant good deed (saying "I love you" to his sister is not enough; clearing the table for her when it is her turn is). If the toy is never rescued, the child has lost interest in it, and it should be given to charity.
- Store small toys carefully. Use a shoe holder with pockets that mounts on the back of a door to store small toys. If they slide out of sight into the pocket, try to find one made of clear plastic.
- Try to do the following in the evening (to avoid the morning rush):

  take baths
  prepare items for school: clothes, lunch money,
    absentee notes
  sign school papers to return
  set table for breakfast

- Divide up the artwork you want to keep for each child as it comes in. Date it, store it in a covered stationery box, and

label the box with the child's name. When that box is full,
sort through it, discarding some treasures for new ones to
come. The best can be slipped into plastic sleeves and kept
in a three-ring binder for the child to keep.

Decision Time—Choose Your Top 20 Percent

This chapter has been full of ideas for the family. Making sure the family functions well, while caring for the demanding needs of children, is complex. Probably your family life doesn't need a complete overhaul, just a few limited, yet important, alterations.

As you read this chapter, perhaps you reacted emotionally to certain parts about being too busy. You may have said, "Yes! That's it! That is definitely my problem!" Or perhaps it was just an "Umm, that's a good idea. I think maybe I will make that change."

As you focus on what will most positively impact your life, look to your emotions, what you are drawn to, your "gut feeling" about what one or two changes will be best for you and your family.

The following are two important changes in our family life that I will try to make:

1.
2.

10

We Are Drowning
in Paper

Get Real about the Paper Problem

Right now, somewhere, someone you've never met is sitting in some corporate office planning to mail you something next week—a catalog, a brochure, a special offer letter. The person planning this mailing is not a bad person; they're just doing their job.

Actually, more likely right now there are twenty people at twenty companies planning to mail you a total of twenty separate items next week.

If you spend just three minutes leafing through each of twenty direct mail offers and catalogs, that's one hour of your week that you will have surrendered to strangers!

Now, if you spend the three minutes reading the letter or the catalog and then you take the next step and save that piece of mail because maybe you'll donate to that cause, or maybe you'll order from that catalog. Add three minutes more per item for filing, stacking, cleaning around, restacking . . .

Think about it: When you hang onto a piece of mail, you've committed at least three minutes of your future time to managing it, whether it's organized or disorganized. You've agreed to take time away from your family, your friends, your job, your community—whatever you really want to be doing—to fool with the written demands of perfect strangers.

How many hours of your life would you like to take back? That depends on how many pieces of mail you can throw away without opening.

Kate S. Brown
Transition Organizers
Annapolis, Maryland
www.transitionorganizers.com

Handling Paper (Ugh!)

A group of library scientists in the 1990s concluded that the total stockpile of information in the world doubled every seven or eight years. A more recent study at the University of California at Berkeley found that in just one year, between 2000 and 2001, the total information in the world doubled.

Obviously, there is no dearth of information in the world. In fact we are drowning in it. This is the information age, and this impacts our desks, offices, and homes, because much of the information ends up in these places in the form of papers that someone sends to us, we print, or we buy.

There are three main reasons we tend to keep too much information:

157

1. *General fear of losing information.* We fear we will need it, so we keep it all—tax forms, bills, contracts. Paper holds a lot of important information we are afraid of losing.
2. *Decision problems.* We fear making a decision about where to put the paper in a file. We want to make the right choice.
3. *Retrieval problem.* We fear losing the paper in a file or pile, so we make lots of little special piles for our special papers.

Face your fears by setting up a system that works for you, asking for outside help if that is possible, and generally tackling the task of handling the papers of your life.

For some who use their computers easily, electronic filing systems may quell a lot of fear of losing papers. Software programs use a Find or Search as part of the system to hone in on the information you are looking for. Check out Kiplinger's Taming the Paper Tiger software. Their promise is "the only guaranteed way to find anything in your home or office in five seconds or less!" Or look into Smead's Arrange software, which encourages us to "find any document in your office with one easy search" and "you'll never lose another file!" Other products of this type will undoubtedly begin entering the marketplace in the future.

You may have to take some time to put the info about your papers into the system, but once it is there, you will be able to find in a jiffy the things you had forgotten you had. A powerful tool!

Is this the Bare Bones Way? As with a few other Bare Bones methods, it may take some time to learn how to use this tool, but once you learn it, your life is greatly simplified.

What Do You Want?

Look at the following reasons people want to improve their handling of paper. Which is most important to you?

- To look better. You want a way to avoid piles and papers stuck in desktop cubbies or jutting out of drawers.
- To find things easily. You want to find things quickly and efficiently, to work with the confidence that you will be able to find what you need when you need it without fail.
- Your image, organizational appearance. Maybe you think you have a good system that works for you. You don't mind the way it looks, and you know where things are even if they don't look very organized. But others complain about your mess. Because of this negative feedback, you want to appear more organized.

How important are these three things to you? Circle the number for each item below.

1	2	3	4	5
Very important		Not important	I want it to look better.	

1	2	3	4	5
Very important		Not important	I want to find things easily.	

1	2	3	4	5
Very important		Not important	I want a better image.	

Once you clearly focus on the benefit you want to achieve, you will work with a stronger resolve to get the job done to your satisfaction.

159

The Bare Bones Way

Paper problems take many forms. In this chapter we will cover several of them:

bills
receipts
files
banking papers
business cards
greeting cards
news clippings
junk mail
notes to yourself
magazines, newspapers, and other subscriptions
appliance manuals
tax papers
school papers

Bills

For most people the highest peak in the paper mountain range in terms of importance is the bills to be paid. For that reason, bills need their own special spot—a drawer, box, cupboard, or some other place. If you designate an easily accessed spot with a container, preferably labeled, from which the bills cannot escape when you are not looking, you will have created the biggest bone, the femur, of the Bare Bones Way.

Then you need a system for keeping up with paying them on time. There are several ways to do this. Put a sticky note on the front of the bill with the due date, write the date on the envelope, obtain a divided day-by-day calendar folder into which the bills go on the day they should be paid, or highlight the due date with a marker when the bill comes in. Perhaps you will develop another system or just shuffle through them on a regular basis to see what needs to be paid.

Make up a simple bookkeeping system in a ledger for keeping track of each regular bill as it arrives monthly (quarterly, or whenever). Somehow, when bills are written down side by side in a systematic way, it's easier to see where the money goes and it is eye-opening.

Another method of paying bills, which many swear by, is online bill paying. You still need to keep up with what is due and when, but it simplifies the mechanics of paying them.

IN THE TRENCHES WITH SMART HOMEMAKERS

From Mary:

I keep my ledger on my computer. I have a template that includes all the regular bills and due dates. At the beginnning of each month I make any necessary changes and additions and print it out. Then it's a handy reference for bill paying on time.

From Karen:

It is pretty important for the bills to have their own place, especially when you bring the mail in. Just place them in there. Include the bills, a pen, stamps, and extra envelopes.

Bills Basket:

I am single and own a home. I have 1 cat (had 2 but one passed on this spring). I used to have a very difficult time finding my bills. I finally got a very nice basket that sits on my computer and holds the bills. Nothing else goes in there. When I get my mail, I open it in front of the shredder. Things I don't want are shredded immediately (I love my shredder, and need to get a new one sometime since this one is wearing out after a year or two of heavy work). Bills go in the basket immediately. Now, I admit, I often forget to pay the bill because I get busy

161

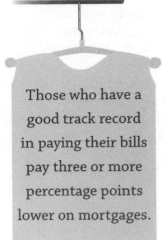

Those who have a good track record in paying their bills pay three or more percentage points lower on mortgages.

with other things but at least I know where the bill is when I do get around to paying it. For me this is an advancement. I used to dump things into Mt Vesuvius boxes and they'd get lost/buried for ages. I managed to pay off a credit card once because it got buried for a year and a half so I couldn't use it.

Slow Bill Paying Solution:

I had a bill paying problem. Money in the bank and just never sat down long enough to write out the checks. Another problem was that if I did them on the dining room table the cats would bother me and make a mess. So I decided to try online bill payment with my checking account. As the bills come in, I try to schedule the payments right away. I can schedule them to be paid by the due date, mark them in my check register and file the paid statement in the bill hanging file. The trick is to do them as they come in.

Prompt Bill Paying and Credit Rating

Paying "in a timely fashion," as they say, is impor-tant to your credit rating. Those who have a good track record pay three or more percentage points lower on mortgages. Credit scoring is used to determine what you pay for insurance and may affect your chances for employment. Most lenders consider a score of 620 to be the lowest acceptable score. Check your credit rating score and note whether there are any errors that need to be corrected. Then set up and use a system to pay your bills promptly, which will raise your score.

Not having money is one thing. Having money and not paying your bills on time is quite another that needs organizational attention. Some payments, such as for insurance or mortgages, can be debited each month automatically from your bank account. Paytrust (www .paytrust.com) is a bill-paying service offered through your bank that can simplify your bill paying. It actually receives your paper bills and then emails you an electronic version. You then authorize payment by a click of your mouse. At the end of the year you can purchase a CD with a summary of your transactions in categories. This system cuts down on paper, saves time, and gives you peace of mind that your bills are being paid. The cost is from five to fifteen dollars per month. For some people it is a way of doing less and getting more—a definite Bare Bones concept.

You can check your credit with the three major credit repositories. It's a good idea to check all three, because they may differ.

- Equifax
  800-685-1111
  www.equifax.com
- Experian
  888-397-3742
  www.experian.com
- TransUnion
  800-888-4213
  www.transunion.com

Check www.creditreporting.com or www.myfico.com for a merged report.

Tips

- To facilitate bill paying, keep everything in one spot you will need for paying bills. This includes stamps, letter opener, envelopes, stapler, pen, and checkbook.
- To start a budget, check out www.financial-education-icfe .org or www.bankrate.com/brm.calc/Worksheet.asp.

Receipts

Receipts fall into two categories, those that come with purchases we make and those from bills.

RECEIPTS FROM STORE PURCHASES

Often store receipts go astray right in the store because they are stuck in the bag, a pocket, or somewhere in your purse. To avoid that problem, consistently follow this system of keeping store receipts.

- If you are a woman and carry a purse, prepare your purse to receive the store receipt. Cut a manila envelope down to the size that will fit into your purse. Make it like a small file folder with a tab. Write RECEIPTS on the tab, and—here is the important part—faithfully file each receipt in the front of the envelope. (If you are a guy, you are on your own on this one.)
- Avoid returning things. Think very, very carefully before bringing anything new into the house. Know before you go the size, dimensions, colors, and the like so you won't need to return things, because returning items takes time. Don't be forced to return things because you buy more than you can afford.
- At the beginning of each month, transfer the receipts from the manila envelope into a shoe box just in case. Then all receipts will be either in your purse file or the shoe box, and they will be in order if you always file to the front. When the shoe box is full, put it in a storage spot. At this point most people will not need to keep the previous box any longer and it can be discarded.

IN THE TRENCHES WITH SMART HOMEMAKERS

From Sue:

I buy & return items often . . . usually I'm returning items because we're needing the money. . . . but, I can never find my receipts (what a wonder!) & so I always feel embarrassed returning. It's usually at Wal-Mart. They will refund your money up to $9.00 without a receipt, so I just make sure I don't have more than $9 worth of stuff to return, or they will give you a gift card if it's more than $9, which is fine because I'll use it to buy groceries.

What I hate is buying an expensive item. Something is wrong with it & I can't find my receipt. I really need to start putting receipts in a central location so I can keep up with them.

RECEIPTS FROM BILLS

When you pay a bill, make a note of the date on the part you keep, which is your receipt. Stack these receipts in the same shoe box you use for the other receipts. At the beginning of each month, add a sheet of paper that indicates the month and year. Now your receipts, which you will not likely ever need again (but fear tells you that you may), are reasonably accessible without a lot of effort on your part.

IN THE TRENCHES WITH SMART HOMEMAKERS

From Shirley:

I have to keep almost all our receipts for hubby's business. I just have a sheet I write them out on (one sheet for each month) divided into categories. Then I just throw all the receipts I've recorded into manila envelopes and clip the paper to the front. Anything like warranties and such goes right in that envelope along with the receipts. When I need a warranty, I just look on the sheet to find out what month we got it, dig through that envelope until I find it. Maybe something like that would work for you? I tried to keep this as simple as I could for myself because I don't like messing around with all these

165

receipts and know I'd put it off till tax day otherwise. We have a lunch bag type cooler that we shove all receipts into until I can get them on the sheets and filed in the envelopes. Lately the cooler has been winning and is overstuffed with receipts, but at least they're all in one place and I can find them if I need them. When hubby needs a receipt or warranty on something he's got on the tow truck, he needs it ASAP or we're losing money. This works well for us.

Files

Ah, here is the tricky part, the part we dread. We don't enjoy opening those file drawers and sticking pages into manila folders. For most of us, it is boring. It is unpleasant. It is scary. It is at this point that the fear mentioned above kicks in. We wonder whether the important piece of paper will ever be found again if it goes into the dark cave of filedom.

As in all organizing, the process begins with categorizing. There are many ways of doing this, most of which work quite well if they make sense to you. The following are the groupings suggested by Marsha Sims of Sort-It-Out.

Papers we want to keep fall into two groups: Action and Reference.

Action

Papers that are temporary, reminding us of things we need to do, are action papers. These include invitations, tickets, reminders from the doctor for a checkup, and the like. Place them in folders that are within reach and store them standing up, perhaps in a small desktop file container available from office supply stores. Some people call this their hot file because it contains items for use in the near future.

166

Indicate what action is required by writing on a sticky note with the sticky part turned to the bottom. Attach the note to the tab of the folder as a sort of temporary file label. Begin with a verb like, Call Doctor or Go to Wedding. When the action is complete, remove the sticky note and discard the materials.

Don't put these papers in a storage filing cabinet drawer unless you have no other place. If you do put them in a file drawer, place the action file in the front of an easily reached drawer.

REFERENCE

Papers we want to keep or store for future use are reference papers. All of the file tabs will begin with a noun, unlike the tabs in the action file, which begin with a verb.

Group your reference papers in the following categories below:

- People. Here you will have a file folder for every member of the family and pets too if you think of them as family members. In each folder will be birth certificate, school records, passport, health information, and other important personal information.
- Places and things. These are papers related to purchases, warrantees, instruction manuals, travel information, decorating, pool information—any information related to tangible items.
- Ideas and interests. Anything you want to save just because you like it, golf, fishing, vitamin research, and the like.
- Financial. Papers having to do with money, such as insurance, AAA, banking, frequent flier, and anything else related to keeping track of money or money-related matters.

- Work related. This may relate to a paid job and be something like contracts. Or it may relate to volunteer work, such as church, garden club, or the library.

IN THE TRENCHES WITH SMART HOMEMAKERS

From Carolyne:

I use file cabinets to keep up with my things. They're not very expensive. Wal-Mart, and lots of other places, sell them. For me, they're a good investment in saved time and energy and peace of mind. I have a big problem with papers. The main one is that I don't like to file. :) So I try to make it as easy as possible. Here are a few ideas that are working for me.

I have a 2 drawer file next to the computer, and another 2 drawer file in a spare bedroom closet.

The first file in the top drawer is for receipts. I can just drop them straight into the file folder, and since it's so accessible, I actually do it. So if I need to return something, the receipt is easy to find. (Which beats my previous system of turning the house upside down, searching for receipts. :)

The second file is local restaurant menus. When I go into town, I can just pull out a menu, call ahead, and save time by picking up food that's ready to go. The file cabinet is right next to the phone, so it's easy to just drop the menu right back into the file.

Financial information—the budget/bills, current living expenses, bank statements, credit card information, savings and debt, insurance, etc., is next, in the top drawer, so that it's easy to get to. Automobile is behind that, then things are alphabetized from there.

At the end of the fiscal year, I take out the financial folders and rotate them to top drawer of the bedroom filing cabinet, and set up new file folders for the new year.

On balancing the checkbook, I usually try to do that the day the checks come in, so it only takes a few minutes, and I don't have to sweat checks bouncing, and those nasty fees. I try to write as few checks as possible, too, which also makes the checking account easier to balance.

I hope this helps someone.

An Alternative View:

I have had filing cabinets coming out my ears (I had a 4 drawer and DD had a 3 drawer). But they never worked for me—it took concentrated time to keep it together.

What has worked though is a concertina file (sometimes called an accordion file) for each member of the family, and one for the "Family" items, and one for the "House" items. I find them easy to use and easy to find things in—and most important, small enough that it is only a little job to go through each year and sort out the paperwork in a short session.

But for on-going stuff, I have beside my desk a pile of letter-sized cardboard envelopes—sort of like manila files with a flap over the top. They have written in big writing along the edge what they hold—bank statements, receipts, medical, bills to pay, etc. And when I am organized, everything gets sorted into that. At the end of the year or 6 months, or as the mood strikes, I sort these into the concertina files. The worst part of the system is the pile that accumulates before putting them in the folders.

The paper fear is a *big* one to calm. I guess one of the most important things I have learned is if you really do not need it—shred it or throw it out.

Banking

Concerning your bank account, I have one wonderful word for you: *Quicken*. I could never balance my checkbook before I got the Quicken program for my computer. Now it takes me about three minutes to reconcile my bank statement. I couldn't live without it now. To "start over" with your account, just don't use it for a couple of weeks till every transaction clears, then use the balance the bank says you have. I can't live without duplicate checks either, especially since I don't carry a check register anymore.

Online banking simplifies keeping up with banking with or without Quicken or any other banking software system.

Online banking simplifies keeping up with banking with or without Quicken or any other banking software system.

Business Cards

It's amazing how many business cards we collect, even if we're stay-at-home moms. Everyone from the telephone repairman to our hairstylist has a business card.

Rolodex files and those of that type are designed to hold business cards alphabetically. Or some people use the computer software called ACT to store all of their business card information. Others scan the cards into the computer. Almost any system is better than the huge random pile with a rubber band around it, or worse yet, with no rubber band.

IN THE TRENCHES WITH SMART HOMEMAKERS

From Aleen:

I have a small album specifically for business cards that I got from an office supply store. Each page has room for 4 business cards (8 if you put them back to back), which go into clear plastic sleeves like a photo album.

I have a page that contains cards for the doctors I go to, one for the vets for my cats, a page with cards for the plumber, electrician, furnace people and cable company, about 3 cards from our favorite restaurants so we can make reservations or call up for delivery. I even have my sisters' business cards from where they work so I can call them during working hours if necessary, and one with my boss' work phone, home phone, and cell phone number if I need to call in.

It sits right next to my telephone and has been quite handy. I add updated or new cards as I get them and very seldom do I lack for an important phone number. If I don't have a card, I cut out a card-sized piece of paper and just write down the information. I like the business cards better than just writing the addresses and phone numbers in an address book because they often list office/open hours, email addresses, and websites.

Greeting Cards

Buy cards for special occasions, either boxed or individually. If they are individually bought, separate them into groups such as get well, birthday, sympathy. Nothing is worse than watching an occasion go by unacknowledged because you didn't have time to purchase a card.

Remember, this organization thing is so you can live your best life. That includes warm relationships with those you care for.

Newspaper Clippings

Cutting out clippings from newspapers and magazines and sending them to friends seems like such a good idea on the face of it. It is sharing knowledge, and knowledge is always good. Right? It is helping others because some of these clippings are very useful. That's good, right? And perhaps, best of all, it is keeping up personal contacts. When you clip an article and send it to someone, it shows you are thinking about the person in a meaningful way. It shows you care. Isn't that very good?

Consider the whole picture. Sharing important information, helping others, and keeping up personal contacts are all wonderful goals when done in the right way. However, the habit of constantly clipping and sending articles can become a bad habit for us to develop.

We are forced to keep and feel guilty about magazines we don't read because of this habit. The pressure to find the right articles, to get them in the mail, perhaps even to file them in case we find someone in need later causes a lot of stress. The space this habit takes up in our house is not as bad as the space it takes up in our heads. The desire to help others in this way can become a very heavy weight.

If you have fallen into the habit of clipping articles, think about whether it is really good for your organizational life. Maybe the first step is to ditch those magazines and newspapers you are saving to go through.

Junk Mail

The best way to solve paper problems is to avoid getting it in the first place. To stop unwanted mail advertising, write the Direct Marketing Association, asking them to remove your name from their direct mailing lists. Within three months 70 percent of the nation's direct marketers will remove your name from their lists, stopping unsolicited mail. Simply send your name, address, and signature with the sentence: "Please remove my name from all solicitation mailing lists." Mail to: Preference Service, Direct Marketing Association, P.O. Box 9008, Farmingdale, NY 11735-9008.

You can also access this service to withdraw and find out more about direct mail by using the web address of the Direct Marketing Association: www.dmaconsumers .org/cgi/offmailinglistdave.

The best comprehensive site I have found is netjunk .com/users/unpretentious/junkmail.html. It contains several more addresses for deletions that are not covered by the address above.

Credit card solicitations are particularly problematic junk mail because we worry that the offer will fall into the hands of someone who will sign up for a credit card in our name. Solicitation for credit cards can be stopped by calling the automated opt out request line, which is 888-5OPT-OUT. I did it and it worked great for me.

You can also get in touch with the individual credit reporting agencies that were listed earlier, asking them to delete your name from credit card solicitation lists. Notice that the phone numbers for stopping unwanted mail are different than those for checking credit.

Equifax Options
Equifax Marketing Decision Systems, Inc.
Box 740123
Atlanta, GA 30374
800-556-4711

Experian (formerly TRW)
Target Marketing Services Division
Attn.: Consumer Opt-Out
P.O. Box 919
Allen, TX 75013
800-353-0809

Trans Union Corporation
Name Removal Option
P.O. Box 7245
Fullerton, CA 92637
800-680-7293

(By the way, to stop unsolicited phone sales calls, call 888-382-1222. This is the do-not-call line.)

Notes and Reminders

Disorganized people seem to make a lot of random notes using little slips of paper, envelopes, paper napkins, whatever, which get misplaced easily. On the other hand, organized people have a systematic note-keeping

system to remember random information, what they want to buy, where they need to go, and so on.

Here are some ideas on how to be more organized with notes and reminders:

Organized people have a systematic note-keeping system to remember random information, what they want to buy, where they need to go, and so on.

• Carry a small notebook in your purse for on-the-go notations and use a phone message book, like those used in offices, to record all information you obtain over the phone.

• Put all of your notations on sticky notes and stick them to a white board mounted on the wall.

• Open a document in your computer. Call it something like INFORMATION JOURNAL and put information into it. You can use the Find or Search button to locate information you have stored there.

Subscriptions

Magazines you have subscribed to but haven't finished reading yet, whether personal or professional, are a great source of stress. They keep piling up. Apparently you don't feel that they are worth your time to read, so you need to discard them.

Here's how:

• Skim them, tearing out articles of interest, and then discard the magazines. This causes the problem of where to put the articles you tear out, but at least they take up less room than the whole magazine.

• Discard the previous issue when a new magazine comes, whether or not you have read it.

• Read only every two or three issues.

174

- Or best of all, call the 800 toll-free number of the subscription offices of the magazine, cancel your subscription, and ask for any refund to which you are entitled. If you must, pick up a copy now and then when you see it on the store rack.

There is no law that says you must take subscriptions of any magazines or newspapers. If you stop your subscriptions, will you really suffer significant loss? Or will their absence be beneficial to you once you get over the shock of not having them around?

Appliance Manuals

You will find appliance manuals in various places as you organize. What will you do with them? There are several ways to keep appliance manuals.

UNDER THE APPLIANCE

One of the best things I have ever done organizationally is to place the manuals under appropriate appliances, especially those that require frequent reference to directions, such as a sewing machine, computer, printer, fax machine, VCR, any appliance that sits on a table, desk, countertop, or the like. All such appliance manuals may be needed for technical assistance.

FILE FOLDER(S)

Storing the manual under the appliance will obviously not work well for large appliances, like stoves or refrigerators. Nor will it work for small electronics, like a handheld calculator, recorder, or CD player. For these, place the manual with the receipt in a folder. The Bare Bones Way is to place all of the guarantees or manuals in one folder.

Another good way is to have a separate folder for each room of the house. Keep all of the room files together in a file cabinet. When you buy an appliance or electronic equipment, staple the receipt to the manual, and place it in the file folder for the room in which the item is located.

The reason for putting the paperwork for appliances in a room folder, rather than in one large folder, is because it simplifies looking for the manual when you are under pressure to find the paperwork. Pressure makes us nervous and it is harder to find needed information. Putting information in smaller, clearly designated groupings makes it easier to find.

NOTEBOOK

Occasionally people use a notebook with plastic sleeves to slip manuals into. Then they label the outside of the notebook and put it on a shelf. This requires more work to set up and use but still is appealing to some.

Tax Papers

Plan for your taxes at the beginning of the year and work that plan all yearlong. Find an easily accessible place for an expandable file envelope. Label the divisions in a way that meets your needs. Write the year on it. Slam-dunk all receipts and information that you will need when you file your tax return into that envelope without fail. Get outside help for doing your income taxes when necessary and ask for the accountant's tips on how to keep organized during the year.

Much difference of opinion exists about how long you need to keep records for legal purposes. Ask somebody whose opinion you respect. You might use as a guide that you need to keep personal tax records for three years under normal circumstances or up to six years if your income has been underreported by 25 percent.

Double-check this information with an appropriate professional.

School Papers

Mothers of school-aged kids face the daily chore of handling papes the kids bring home. Such papers fall into various categories and require different methods of handling. The way to decide how to handle them is by looking at what we need them for.

- Papers you will need soon. Keep a desktop file with each child's name on labeled hanging folders in a convenient place. This is where you should file all papes that need to be returned, signed, or that give information about date-related events such as the fall festival or upcoming parent conferences. In all files, always file to the front. Make a note of any dated information on a calendar next to the desktop file. The secret is to devise a plan and use it consistently.
- Papers for storage. Report cards, progress reports, art work, and even things like medical reports should be be kept in a folder for each child for each year as mentioned under information about files. Subdivide into categories as you see the categories develop.
- For the kids to use. Kids need file folders, cubbies, or a desk system of some kind to keep up with daily and long-term homework. When the work is done, put it in the book bag and station it at the door.

Decision Time—Choose Your Top 20 Percent of Paperwork

Paper is ubiquitous. Paper problems are myriad. To begin to get your mountain of paper under control, focus

177

on just one or two areas. This chapter has hit some of the most prevalent paper-handling problems. You may want to begin with some of these. In the list below, put a 1 beside the two areas you feel will bring you the most relief if they are changed. After you have chosen two, write beside them what you will do to begin to get this area under control. Work on accomplishing these objectives. Come back to the others, if you wish, after you have done the first two.

____ Bills. I will:

____ Receipts. I will:

____ Files and filing cabinets. I will:

____ Banking. I will:

____ Business cards. I will:

____ Greeting cards. I will:

____ News clippings. I will:

____ Junk mail. I will:

____ Notes and reminders. I will:

____ Subscriptions. I will:

____ Appliance manuals. I will:

____ Tax papers. I will:

____ School papers. I will:

11

Closets Set the Tone for the House

Organizing Closets

Every closet in your home should be assigned a specific, unique function. First, go through your home/office/apartment and give each closet its "job." Then, one closet at a time, go through and remove any items not related to its newly assigned function. As you clean, create three boxes for the outgoing clutter: donation, throwaway, and sell. One tactic I suggest is to remove everything in the closet first, and sort items as you are putting them back. (Make sure you give yourself enough time to complete the task. It takes at least 2–4 hours for a coat closet, if fully packed, and 4–8 hours for a fully packed bedroom closet.) But before putting everything away, stop and ask yourself: Does the closet need painting? Airing out? Vacuuming? Do you want to install another shelf?

Repair the rod? How about adding another hanging bar and increasing your short hanging space? Or robe or hat hooks on the internal walls or door? Do you need a shoe rack? Is there enough lighting?

Once you have matched the contents to their assigned closets, you are one step closer to making items easier to locate when you need them. Next, put your most frequently used items near the front of the closet—this is your Ergonomic Storage. Store items that are rarely used in the backs of closets or in areas that are harder to reach—this is your Seasonal Storage. Also remember to group "like items" together within the closet, like sports equipment, cleaning products, or hats and gloves.

Meg Connell
Estate, Corporate, and Residential Organizing
Oakland, California
www.theorganizedone.com

Cleaning closets can be a tricky business. Good plans can go downhill quickly. You start out with high resolve to do the deed that you've been putting off. You lay the clothes out on the bed for examination and pull out shoes with other items that somehow found their way into the recesses of the shelves.

But then you get a phone call, grab a bite of lunch, empty the dishwasher, go pick up the kids, stop by the store, help with homework, and, exhausted, move the clothes off the bed and fall in it.

This is the story day after day until the would-be closet cleaner and the clothes are worn out from the constant moving back and forth.

What Do You Want?

There are several kinds of closets. Put a check beside the closets in your house the most in need of change.

___ utility closet—which one?

___ clothes closet—which one?

___ linen closet

___ pantry or food closet

The Bare Bones Way

Utility Closets

Tangled extension cords, lightbulbs, picture-hanging kits, these are the things that go into a utility closet. I have a super idea for organizing the utility closet, and I want to share it with you: Use clear plastic boxes. They may be shoe boxes with detachable tops or drawers that pull out. I have about thirty in my closet. They are wonderful. When I first cleaned out the utility closet, I found that the items to be put away were falling into categories. So I bought plastic boxes (frequently on sale during dollar days at variety and drug stores) and later drawer systems of a size that fits on shelves. On the outside of the boxes and drawers into which I deposited the groups of items, I attached a card naming the various categories. The labels on my boxes include:

- Shoe things (polishes, laces, brushes)
- Repair stuff (light switch plates, wall plugs, etc.)
- Curtain hardware (hooks for curtains, plastic balls for the pull cords, curtain rod brackets)
- Tape, ribbons, and strings
- Lightbulbs
- Soap, toothpaste, and emery boards
- First aid items

181

Remember, the boxes must be clear plastic and the category must be put on the front either with plastic tape and a labeling gun or with tabs used for labeling in a filing system.

If you store mops or brooms in the utility closet, buy clamps and attach them to the wall. Awkward things like irons and ironing boards can be stored with special holders designed to keep them off the floor. Try to keep the floor as bare as possible. It's easier to keep clean that way and looks much neater.

IN THE TRENCHES WITH SMART HOMEMAKERS

From Penelope:

I have recently had the house renovated and had to move out in order for workmen to get the job done. Soon after I moved back in, a friend loaned me a copy of *The New Messies Manual*.

Less than a week later I gave her back her copy and bought my own. I have been bringing things back into the house gradually so that I do not get overwhelmed and am trying to find homes for everything before I bring the next box in. This is not proving to be as easy as it sounds, however your "centers" idea, the labeling and the boxes ideas have proved to be very useful. Recently I established an "Electrical box" in which I keep extension cords, double adapters, lightbulbs, batteries, insulation tape and a flash light. It will soon have fuse wire, wire cutters, and pliers in it. The box is clear plastic and I have used a Dymo labeler to list the contents on the outside including the location of an extra long extension cord.

Twice lately I have been asked if I had a double adapter and once for a light bulb. I was able to find them all within seconds—in the past I was always buying new ones because I couldn't find the ones I had already. Thank you so much for your book and the ideas in it. I dread to think what things would be like without them.

An Organizer in Process:

I have made a little progress in my bedroom this morning but, of course, the bed itself is full. I organized a small storage closet for health and beauty items, which enables me to actually put some of this sort of thing away instead of poking through my assortment of lumpy bags because "I know it's in here somewhere!" This will be a great relief.

Try to keep the floor as bare as possible. It's easier to keep clean that way and looks much neater.

Clothes Closets

Why are closets such a problem? Many closets are too small for all we want to put in them. However, if you look at your closet, you will see a lot of wasted space, usually below the hanging clothes and above the clothes rod.

COMMERCIAL CLOSET SYSTEMS

The logical solution for closets that have only one bar is to install two bars, one above the other, thus making better use of more space in the closet. To put in two bars, the top bar needs to be raised. Carmen, my Cleanie friend, did this by taking out all the wood shelves and bars and replacing them with plastic coated, ventilated wire shelving. There are three advantages to this type of shelving:

1. You can see what is on the high shelf more easily through the spaces between the wires.
2. Less dusting is required, since there is no solid shelf.
3. You can use the front rod of the shelf as a hanging bar; the wires attached to the rod hold the clothes hangers apart evenly.

183

You can find these shelving systems in many stores that carry closet hardware. There are closet companies that will install them for you if you cross their palms with silver. Look under *closet* in the Yellow Pages.

DO-IT-YOURSELF CHANGES

Now suppose you say, "That's too big a job for right now. What can I do with my closet the way it is?" Let me tell you my situation. If it requires a hammer and nails and takes more than five minutes to do, I don't do it. My husband and I are not handy with building things, and the few occasions when I have had someone do it for me have been somewhat unsatisfactory. So I look for easy-to-install ready builts. In this case I add another shelf to the top of the closet by supporting it with some kind of prop to make use of the empty space up there. Of course, that shelf will be pretty much out of reach so I will use it to store only seldom used things. You can utilize the space at the bottom of the closet by obtaining a low drawer system that fits whatever space is unused.

An easy-to-install lower bar can be hung from the bar above in various ways. Check catalogs for useful products, or obtain a PVC plastic tube, cut to an appropriate length. Attach it to the bar above at each end with a rope threaded through the tube. Having a low bar in the children's closets helps them get in the hang-up habit too.

There are other good methods for organizing your closet. Don't let the shoes make your closet a mess. The back of the closet door is invaluable space for storage systems designed to hold shoes, belts, ties, and some jewelry. If you make your closet an organizing project (after you have finished discarding excess, of course), look for ideas in closet organizing books, articles, or on the Internet.

CLOTHES HANGERS

An important element of clothing storage that is often overlooked is the clothes hanger. Get rid of the wire hangers, buy plastic tubular ones instead, and be sure to have enough for all your clothes. One reason people don't hang up their clothes is because it is so hard. Sometimes there aren't enough hangers. The wire coat hangers hook over each other, making them hard to take out. Frequently the wire hangers with the round cardboard tube given out by cleaners are broken in the middle of the tube when we get them out, which discourages hanging up pants. And then, of course, there is the problem of too many clothes in the closet, which makes getting something in or out a tug-of-war.

Let me mention that you can pick up the plastic tubular hangers at many dollar day sales or buy a few each time you go to the store. Don't wait too long to get them, though. Buy one color of hanger; brown is good because it is stylish and somewhat neutral.

I suggest you paint your closet white and keep it that way so you won't have to repaint it each time you paint the bedroom. Can you envision that beautiful neat closet with the white walls and brown hangers? Looks good, doesn't it?

ORGANIZING THE CLOTHES

The best color-coding application I have ever made is with my clothing. I divided my clothes into four groups: slacks, blouses, two-piece outfits, and dresses. In each group I arranged the clothes from light to dark, like an artist's palette. This did wonders. Previously, I could not tell whether the pair of slacks I was looking for was out of the closet or in the closet, lost under something. Now I know that if my black slacks are not right at the end of the slacks section, they are not in the closet. This trick also helps me see the clothes I have and how I can mix and match them. I highly recommend this system.

DECLUTTER THE CLOTHES CLOSET

Perhaps in no other area are we more tempted to keep unused things than in the clothes closet. We have things too big or too small in case we gain or lose weight. We have things that are good but that we never wear because we don't like them. But they are good—that is, they fit and the buttons are on. So we have to keep them—especially if we paid a lot for them. We keep out-of-style things we used to love, just in case the style returns. It seldom does and never in the same way. Sometimes we keep a dress that is out of style because the skirt could be made into something nice. We never get to that project; but if we ever do, we will have that wonderful dress to work with.

The worst reason to keep clothes cluttering up our closets is that we are keeping them in case someone else would like them. Sometimes we don't have a specific person in mind, so we keep them until we locate somebody who would profit from our generosity. Being perfectionists, we have to make sure it is just the perfect person. So we put the clothes aside until we get around to sending them to cousin Mary's boy. He'll probably have a son of his own before we get them in the mail!

Listen, let's quit dreaming. We are not going to do the alterations. We are not going to gain or lose weight while the style is still in. If we do, we can reward ourselves with new clothes. Don't wait for the perfect person to wear the outfit you are saving. Give it to the nearest charity. Let them find the perfect person.

IN THE TRENCHES WITH SMART HOMEMAKERS

A Closet Organizer from Australia:
Yesterday, I determined that I needed to be able to use all my closet. Always in the past, when I have tackled an organizing, cleaning project, it has seemed like it looked worse afterward than when I began. I would always pull everything out and get completely overwhelmed and even though I might get "close" to finishing, I never could actually finish. This time it was different. Armed with the knowledge that I must *not* pull out more than I could deal with effectively and that I absolutely must *not* quit until I had accomplished my goal, *I did it*. I determined that all I wanted to do was to make a path to the other side of the closet. I pulled out just what I needed to and dealt with it as I went along. I just kept plugging along until I got the area looking nice. It was highly motivating and I really hated to stop and go to bed.

Storage Closet Success:
Yesterday, I spent 15 minutes in mine and DD's shared walk-in closet. It was by far the worst room in the house. I started by organizing the shoes, DD's on her side and mine on my side. Then I picked up all of the clothes off of the floor and put them in the dirty laundry (which, by the way I finished before 8 o'clock this morning).

I only spent 15 minutes in there, but it already looks presentable!

Linen Closets and Pantries

Organizing linens in closets and food in pantries follows the same pattern as organizing other closets. Here are some things to remember:

- Set aside a specific time to organize the closet. Motivation and determination are key ingredients of a successful project. If possible, work with a helper. Having support makes the job so much easier.

187

- Group similar items together. Use those white boxes mentioned earlier to keep items corralled while you are pulling things off the shelves and grouping them. Gather up items around the house that should be in the closet you're working on and put them in the appropriate group.

- After you have completed gathering similar items, discard duplications. Nobody needs ten glue sticks or whatever you find you have bought in excess because you couldn't find what you needed at the time you needed it. Evaluate how much room each bunch will need. Return the groupings to the shelves, always placing the most used items within easy reach. Where reasonable, place small items, like food packets or small boxes, into plastic square baskets or plastic shoe boxes.

- When everything has been properly stowed, identify the grouping with a label, either on the side of the basket or on the shelf. Write the category on an index card (my favorite way) or use a high-tech label maker. A label will help keep things from wandering out of place, which they tend to do, especially at night when you are not looking. When items are grouped appropriately in closets, you and your family will be able to locate what you need and, more important, will know exactly where items go when you're finished with them.

- Attack only the amount of reorganizing you have time to finish. If you miscalculate and run out of time, put the tops on the boxes and set them aside temporarily. This leaves no messy overflow from the half-finished job to mess up the rest of the house.

Tips

- Clear the closets using the three *C*s: consolidate, containerize, and condense. If you choose to empty the closet entirely to begin afresh or to paint it, be sure you have enough time to do it completely in one session. Commandeer a friend and set a time schedule.

   As you empty clothes, have three piles: YES, NO, and MAYBE. If you have boxes for the last two categories, you can move the MAYBE items into temporary storage while you decide and the NO items out of the house quickly.
- Store shoes in shoe bags on back of the door or on wire or wood shoe racks on the floor or closet shelf. Very dressy shoes or shoes seldom worn can be kept in their original shoe boxes labeled on the outside.
- Don't let empty hangers dangle between hangers with clothes on them. Have a spot at the end of the rod or on a shelf for the hangers that are not in use.
- No room in the linen closet? Store seldom used sheets between the box spring and the mattress.
- Need another shelf in the closet but have no room? Put a shelf inside the closet above the door for seldom used items.
- To avoid crowding your closet with too many clothes that don't match, choose two or three colors and coordinate each purchase around those. Don't buy anything that doesn't match three other items you already have.

Decision Time—Choose Your Top 20 Percent for Closet Organizing

Closets can absorb in an orderly fashion what would be disorder if left out in the open. Because of this function, they can set the tone for the whole house. When it comes to organizing, closets are places where you can be tempted to overdo, to drag everything out at once and "go to it." Eventually all your closets will need to be overhauled and upgraded into storage units of maximum usefulness. But for now, keeping in mind the choices you made in the What Do You Want? section of this chapter and using your gut feeling for what will make the biggest difference with the least time and effort, name three actions you can take at this time to improve your closets. Later you can work at reorganizing all your closets.

1.
2.
3.

Garages, Basements, Attics, Sheds, and Other Neglected Storage Areas

A Clearer View of Garages

With dampness and temperature fluctuations, the garage, attic or basement is not the best place to store many items. Add the inevitable dirt, dust, and critters, and those valuables can become not so valuable. In practice, these storage spaces often become a catchall for the things we don't have the guts

Rightly done, the garage can be very useful for storage as well as a home for the car.

to part with. What goes on in our minds when we store useless things in the garage, and our $40,000 investment is parked unprotected on the street or driveway? Hmm, sounds like prime real estate is going to waste! Yet, these spaces have great potential for storage, when we make the most of the space and store appropriate items there.

Mary Lynn Murray
It's About Time Organizing Services
Walnut Creek, California
www.marylynnmurray.com

Americans love cars. They also love the space cars are supposed to fit in—the garage. Ninety-seven percent of all new homes come with an attached garage. Three-car garages are fast replacing two-car garages as the size of choice.

Sometimes all or part of the garage is used for an overflow family room, a rock band studio, a home office, an exercise room, or many other activities. In today's world, overloaded as it is with possessions, one of the main uses of the garage is as a large storage unit. Rightly done, the garage can be very useful for storage as well as a home for the car.

Ideally, we will store things only on the walls and ceiling of the garage. Sometimes the walls are lined with shelves to hold items. In many garages one "stall" of the garage is dedicated to a purpose other than the car, such as storing bicycles, exercise equipment, or mowers. And woe be to the family whose garage is so full of items that the car won't fit in, they are unable to enter, and nothing is accessible. That kind of situation is a containerized trash heap. If you've got it, you need to face it in the Bare Bones fashion.

Basements and attics, like garages, are significant storage areas. However, they are often used as places to stash items about which we postpone decisions. Definitely not a good idea. Later we are forced to go back and make hard choices about a lot of things we should have cared for one at a time.

What Do You Want?

When you tackle the storage area, what do you want to do? (check all that apply):

____   Get rid of a lot of the stuff.
____   Organize and label what's there for easier access.
____   Move the things to another area.
____   Make significant change, such as be able to get the car in the garage or use the basement as a playroom.
____   Clean the area.

The Bare Bones Approach

Things have gotten out of hand, way out of hand! Treasure, trash, and maybe critters live together in the garage. The job may have gotten too big for you to handle alone. Depending on the situation, you may need to follow a plan similar to the one below.

1. Start early in good weather. This is going to be a long job. Spring and fall are good times of year to tackle a garage.
2. Get help. Ask a family member, neighborhood teen(s), professional organizer or housecleaner, or any other resource you can think of if you really try. If you give someone decision-making

privileges (such as where to put stuff and what to throw away), be sure you communicate clearly your guidelines for how to handle your things.

IN THE TRENCHES WITH SMART HOMEMAKERS

From Susie:

Dear, dear Ladies,

When you work full time, have a household to run, have children, spend 2 1/2 hours commuting, have a debilitating illness/are coming back from one, are in mourning, &/or you have special caretaking responsibilities (frankly, any one of these), for goodness' sake, it's okay to need help, and, Guess what? Professional housecleaners will understand!! You *deserve* a hand with getting things under better control! It sounds as if y'all think there's something wrong with you, that you can't be three (healthy) people all rolled into one!

Sure, it may be really embarrassing to expose how bad things have gotten, but it would be really worse if you *didn't* get help and you and your family had the ongoing drag-coefficient of a house-out-of-control on top of everything else. *That's* debilitating. The disarray won't go away by itself, &, with all the other things y'all are dealing with, you are perfect candidates for housecleaning assistance. *Please,* don't let mere embarrassment keep you from getting a hand. As L'Oreal says, "You're worth it!" So is your family, and so are those husbands who aren't getting time with their wives because the house stands in the way.

You can always explain to the prospective housecleaners that things have gotten out of control in your home and that you're not expecting miracles overnight, but you need help to start whittling away at the backlog. You will not be the first family they've worked for who needed this help. I hope those of you who are only holding off on getting help because of embarrassment will love yourselves enough to do it anyway.

I am a sadder but wiser mom of grown children. I never realized my own value until my children's childhoods were over. They missed out on so many experiences because I was always trying to get mastery of the house by myself. I would have been so much better off getting over the shame and getting assistance with housecleaning, so my kids could have the *best* parts of me.

Susie, with love for all of us who have dreams to fulfill

Continuing with the plan:

3. Decide on a disposal system. Have a truck haul things away or use some other kind of disposal service. You will probably give some things away, throw away some, and keep some (go easy on this one), so you will need to make arrangements to handle these different categories. If you're getting rid of items, do it as soon as possible—preferably on the day of the project.

   You may decide to sell some items. If you are going to have a garage sale, obtain containers, labeling each with a price, and deposit items into them as you clean your garage. In other words, price them as you go by grouping like priced items together. Then later you won't have to go back through the things to decide on prices. Some people then just sell the things right out of the box. Others display them in groups according to price.

   Before you start the garage-cleaning project, set a date for the sale. Make it close to the cleaning day. Otherwise, it is easy just to let the garage sale items sit in boxes indefinitely, and they may even become a starter for a new collection of junk. Whatever is not sold should be boxed and transferred to your nearest charity. Notice I did not say your "dearest" charity. Unless you have compelling reasons to do otherwise, your stuff needs to move swiftly out of your life, preferably on the afternoon the sale ends.

4. Plan a storage system for what you keep, using the principles of the three Cs. Before you begin your organizing project, have a storage plan and materials in place.

5. Take care of yourself while you are cleaning the garage. Plan lunch, have plenty of drinks available, and in the evening, have a preplanned, wonderful meal waiting in the slow cooker smelling great for you and your helpers. Maybe even set the table before you start the job.

IN THE TRENCHES WITH SMART HOMEMAKERS

From Gail:

I went out to my garage to put a few pieces of counter clutter away yesterday and saw a shambles. My garage is trashed! Why? Well, every single thing I looked at that was a mess is a mess because

a. I didn't take the time to put it away properly.
b. There is no proper way to put the stuff away, so I just let it sit there.
c. I abandoned a project part way through.
d. I didn't clean up after myself (packing paper all over the floor).
e. Stuff is piled up waiting for "just in case"—empty useful containers, which I will probably, or *might* need later.

So, right now, I'm melting down in a puddle of frustration. I'm grumpy, I'm mad, I'm . . . everything! Grrrrr! I'm also probably under the influence of hormones, but that's just served to bring this all out in the open instead of letting me ignore it.

Last night I just wanted to start tossing stuff out into the driveway, all night! When the inevitable people drove by asking if it was a garage sale, I'd just say, *Yes, take it all for free!! Thieves, help yourselves!!*

So, the first thing I'm doing this morning, now that I've reached the limit of sitting still, is to put together a notebook of all this diet stuff I've been working on (for a new yahoo group and for dh [dear husband] and myself). Then I'm going to do some long overdue cleaning while making notes on all the whirling declutter thoughts in my head, and then my neighbors better *duck* because by the time my family goes camping at the end of the month, I'm going to have made some changes to this cluttery mess!! Arrrgh!!

From Cheryl:
All the donation fabric I put into my yard sale last May was still hanging around the garage, and today I took it to a good home—a church that makes all kinds of fabrics into quilts. I *know* I should have gotten rid of it sooner and that I shouldn't have had the mental block against letting it go no matter what was going to happen to it later, but this makes me happy. Not so much that "my" fabric is going to a "good home," but that resources aren't being wasted. Is that a touch of the Idealistic Messie coming out in me? LOL

So, my garage is getting emptier and emptier. I have a donation pickup scheduled for next week, and they'll even take it out of my garage if it is near the front and labeled and the door is open. No problem! I can stack it and cordon it off so that it can be considered gone already. I may even really truly be able to get a car in there, but maybe not by Sept. 30. We'll see.

Big progress! Woo hoo!

Tips for Garages

- Try to keep the floor free of clutter; do not use floors for storage.
- Use the ceiling (all those handy beams and joists) to hang up bicycles, lawn chairs, tire rims, backpacks, and other light, bulky items. Hardware stores sell large, vinyl covered hooks for this purpose.

- Use the walls to hang up smaller items or items you need more often. Nail a piece of Peg-Board to the exposed studs in the garage and use *S* hooks to hang up gardening equipment, tools, and sports gear.
- Keep a large piece of heavy cardboard (an old refrigerator box, for example) on the floor of the garage where you park your car. It will catch any oil or antifreeze drips that would stain the floor (concrete is very porous, and, besides, the color of the drips will help you know what fluid is leaking).
- Invest in shelves, cabinets, or other storage units.
- Label jars to hold nails, screws, washers, and other small parts.
- If you recycle trash, keep labeled garbage cans or large boxes in an easily accessible area of the garage and enlist the help of family members in using and emptying them regularly.
- Practice fire prevention 365 days a year. Get rid of piles of newspapers, old paint cans, and oily rags, especially around furnaces or in unventilated areas. There are less drastic ways to rid your life of clutter than burning the house down!

The Bare Bones Approach for Basements and Attics

Like the garage, the basement and attic that have not been transformed into finished rooms are not generally climate controlled. What is stored in them is often subject to heat, cold, and moisture. Unlike the garage, which is often used as an entryway to the house and therefore often visible, the attic is seldom seen and the basement, unless it houses laundry equipment, is also out of sight.

In most homes, the attic is the least accessible area. Move seldom used items, heirlooms, and light things that are easy to carry upstairs to the attic. Because heat rises, it is probably hotter and dryer than the basement, and the basement may be more subject to flooding.

Taking these factors into consideration, the basement and attic should be organized in the same way the garage is, using the three Cs. However, when these three steps are finished, one more step is helpful.

Because things stored in these areas are seldom seen and seldom or never used, they can be forgotten or even "lost." A dearly loved children's tea set, which had been saved for the first little granddaughter, may disappear into the black hole of forgetfulness only to emerge years later at an estate sale long after the little one's teatimes are over.

To avoid this problem, do not only number and label boxes in large, clear letters, noting what resides therein, but also make a master list of what is in each numbered box. Put the list near the storage area in an obvious place such as right inside the door or taped to the inside of the attic or basement door. Keep a copy either on a paper or on 3 × 5 cards, one card for each box, with your other papers. You may want to keep a list on your computer so you can use the Find or Search button to locate an item you need. But of course, computers come and go and cards get lost. However, that yellowing list hung by the attic entrance will be a gold mine of information for years to come.

Decision Time—Choose Your Top 20 Percent

As you know, the premise of this book is to focus activity on the areas of your house that will produce the best results, leaving the rest undone, at least for now. Of the storage areas mentioned in this chapter, which one would be most helpful to improve?

_____ garage

_____ attic

_____ basement

_____ other areas such as shed, utility room, out-
house (no, not that kind!), or barn

In the area you chose, what is the least you can do to bring about significant change? Chucking an old bike, broken lawn mower, bent golf clubs, or some such thing? Chucking all three of these plus the rusted out barbecue grill will really make a difference! Will purchasing new shelving do the trick? Or reboxing? Or placing hooks or grids for hanging? How about discarding one or two boxes? Is there some other little thing you have been meaning to do but haven't yet? Do it today.

Let's face the facts. If you are going to do a drastic reorganizing job on any one of these areas, there is no way to make any of these projects simple. So we need to give serious consideration to the question of what can be done to bring about the biggest benefit. If only a serious reorganization is reasonable in the light of your need, make plans to do it all as quickly and easily as possible in one day using adequate help.

My plan is to:

13

Living Safely with the Laundry Glacier

Basics of Laundry 101

We have gone into a lot of chronically disorganized homes and found laundry, laundry, laundry everywhere. One of our jobs as a professional organizer is to help our clients solve their laundry problems.

The very first thing we have to tackle is making sure they have places to handle all the parts of doing their laundry. Now for some of you this may sound obvious, but in some houses it is not easy.

The washer and drier are in a location that does not have the ability to handle the laundry when it is done. Therefore it is

Laundry is not brain surgery. Just do it!

spread all over the house. Clothes wrinkle when not folded or hung soon after leaving the dryer, and wrinkled clothes mean more work for our clients and more of a mess.

We try to find spare space, be it in a spare bedroom or garage, where the clothes can be taken right from the dryer so they can be hung, folded, or placed in individual laundry baskets for each member of the household to take to their rooms and put away.

A lot of the solution is in taking the time to find and set up workable locations to do the job.

Pat Rabon
A to Y Organizing
Missouri City, Texas
AtoYorganizing.com

Laundry (along with paperwork) is the biggest specific complaint of housewives. It is like an avalanche that keeps coming, over which we feel we have little control. Or maybe it is more like a glacier, slow and inexorable in its buildup on a daily basis. We have some flexibility and control over food preparation or cleaning or organizing—but laundry seems to have a mind of its own.

However, we do have power beyond what we suppose if we break out of old ideas and habits and set up better systems to channel that avalanche into a manageable stream.

Perfectionism can be a hindrance in doing laundry. Many people are hung up by trying to sort just the right pieces together, making sure the wash load is full to save detergent and water for protection of the environment, and many other ideas that hinder moving forward easily and quickly. Laundry is not brain surgery. Just do it!

You will hear it again and again from those who do it without difficulty—laundry is one continuous process. The more quickly it is done from beginning to end, the better. Most folks don't have trouble actually washing and drying the clothes because machines do most of the work. However, many people get hung up on returning clean and folded clothes to where they belong. No machine will do this. The main thing to remember is that the job is not done until the clothes are put away.

Where Are You?

Mark the spot on the line that seems to represent where you are between the two extremes:

1	2	3	4	5
I feel inundated by laundry.			Laundry is well under control and no bother to me.	

1	2	3	4	5
I have piles of clean laundry waiting to be folded.			I fold and put away laundry as it is dried.	

1	2	3	4	5
I have no special plan for laundry.			I have and implement a plan to limit the use of clothes, towels, etc.	

1	2	3	4	5
I do laundry irregularly as needed.			I have a schedule that moves laundry along regularly.	

1	2	3	4	5
Clothes that need to be ironed are a problem.			Ironing is no problem.	

1	2	3	4	5
I buy what I like regardless of care instructions.			I look carefully at care instructions before buying.	

203

1	2	3	4	5
My clothes get very wrinkled in the wash.			I am careful to prevent wrinkles in the wash.	

1	2	3	4	5
Often folded clothes are not put away immediately.			I put folded clothes away quickly.	

Laundry—the Bare Bones Way

"How can you write about washing and ironing?" my husband asked. "You don't do either."

Bingo!

That is the heart of the Bare Bones Way—wear clean and unwrinkled clothes while working as little as possible—maximum benefit from minimum effort.

How do I do it? There are several factors. I generally buy clothes that wash easily and don't need ironing, most of them anyway. We have a three-bin laundry hamper. My husband washes the clothes. (He has a weird system of sorting but I don't complain.) His style is to do small loads almost daily. He hangs clothes wet on hangers (we have no electric dryer) and I put all of them, even if they need ironing, in the closet when they are dry.

He washes the whites and hangs them on the line to dry. I fold them and put them away when he brings them in.

I have one or two garments that need dry cleaning. Recently I was lured into buying cute, springy cottons that require ironing. Believe me, I learned my lesson! I now take a public vow to avoid that temptation ever again. Ironing them is a real nuisance. No more cottons that need ironing for me!

Laundry can be divided into specific steps. Work a plan for each step and the laundry problem melts like a bar of soap in a puddle.

1. *Start solving problems early in the process.* Buy easy-care clothes, bedclothes, and table linens. If you want to afford it, dry cleaning offers an easy way to get clothes clean, that is, if the cleaner is easily accessible. Whatever you do, think ease of care before you buy.

2. *Limit clothes and linen use.* Wear clothes as many times as possible between washings. People often drop worn but unsoiled clothes in the laundry hamper rather than deal with what to do with once-worn clothes. One suggestion is to put these lightly worn clothes carefully into a discreetly placed slush pile to be used at the first occasion in the future. Some people hang them in a special place in the closet. Still others turn the coat hanger hooks in the backward direction and return them to the closet among their clean clothes. (I hear some of you perfectionists gasp at this point.) These last folks keep an eye (and nose) out for soil problems in this process.

Towels can be big offenders when it comes to over-washing. It is easy to fall into the habit of using too many. Some families limit themselves to one towel and washcloth per person per week. Sometimes, this needs modifying. But always there needs to be a reasonable limitation or you will turn into a slave to washing, folding, and putting away towels.

The average length of time people use their sheets between washings is two weeks. The people who seem to be most satisfied with their sheet washing plan are those who strip the bed, wash, dry, and return those same sheets to the bed the same day. That way they don't have to fold or store an extra pair of sheets.

3. *Develop a system.* Most people have a basic approach for washing that works for their water type and lifestyle. They have a few products and basic settings on the washer and dryer that are their stock-in-trade. For the most part, using this approach works pretty well. The problem comes in the timing of the steps—laundry back-

ing up because it is done too seldom or sporadically. The best thing is to get a system, such as the one described here that was followed by one particular family.

Each day the wife puts laundry in to wash before she leaves for work. She includes softeners to avoid wrinkles. Her husband puts them into the dryer when he comes home before she does. She arrives in time to get them out before they wrinkle. She folds and hangs them, putting each person's clothes on a hanger or in a dishpan with the person's name on it in the laundry room. She puts away her clothes and the folded linens, and the job for the day is done. Family members retrieve and put away their own clothes.

Obviously, this plan is specific to this family, but it could work for you, or your plan may be entirely different as are the following:

- Janet washes only three loads a week for herself and her husband. Two loads are clothes and one is linens. For her, laundry is a nonproblem. She washes and dry-cleans her "good" clothes as seldom as possible, lightly wearing them ten or fifteen times before they need attention. "See this jacket," she asked, flapping the collar of what she was wearing. "It has never been cleaned and I have worn it many times." She hand washes rayon clothes, which call for dry cleaning, wraps them in a towel to absorb the excess water, fluffs out the wrinkles in the dryer, and hangs them damp to finish drying. They seldom need any ironing.
- Karen and her husband have five children. She pays one child to do all the laundry. The dried laundry is placed in a basket and a block with a family member's name is placed in the basket on a rotating basis. It's this person's job to fold the laundry.

If the laundry is not folded before dinner by the person whose name is on the block, he or she does it the next time as well.

- Lucy has trained her two boys to do their own laundry, and she takes care of the rest.
- Ramona takes her clothes to a local laundry, which will do the washing and drying for her. She figures it costs about five dollars more a week and saves her a couple of hours. She likes the tradeoff, and besides, they fold more neatly than she does.

> The worst approach is no plan, washing only when the hampers overflow and nobody has any underwear left to wear.

The varieties of plans are myriad. The worst approach is no plan, washing only when the hampers overflow and nobody has any underwear left to wear. Often, using this plan, wash is sorted into Mount Washmores all over the floor waiting to be done. Later, the huge piles of dried (and wrinkling) laundry sit on the sofa or in baskets waiting for a marathon folding session, which is usually slow in coming. The job is mammoth. The mess is too and so is the resistance to doing such a huge job.

4. *Hang unironed clothes in the closet and put unironed linens on the shelf where they belong.* Iron clothes as needed or at a designated ironing time.

5. *Do laundry without emotion.* Become a robot and just follow your plan mechanically.

IN THE TRENCHES WITH SMART HOMEMAKERS

From Sandra J.:

I keep only one hamper in the bedroom—it is relatively small, so it holds only 2–3 days of soiled clothes (for the two of us).

I take the hamper to the laundry room, and as I pull the clothes out I sort them into a triple bag laundry sorter. As each section of the sorter becomes full, I do that load (whites, mixed, black, etc). For me it means a load every day, which I wash before dinner and dry after dinner.

Every item goes on a hanger as it comes out of the dryer (we have a wooden dowel mounted below a shelf next to the dryer) or into a basket to go into the drawers (one basket for his and one for mine). He (hubby) takes his basket and hangers to the bedroom. I have arranged the wash schedule so that his work clothes are done on Thursday, so that Sunday night there isn't a scramble at midnight to get his black socks done! Not anymore.

Towels have their own hamper in the bathroom. When towels or sheets come out of the dryer, they are piled in a chair in the LR for me to fold while watching TV. Fortunately, our linen closet is in the hall next to LR so it's a short walk to finish the job. I usually do towels and sheets on the weekend, because I can start a load before we go out for recreation and it doesn't matter if they sit in the washer or dryer all day. Don't get me wrong, I still have to work hard against my natural tendencies, but at least I have a plan to attempt to follow; and it works most of the time. Hope these ideas help someone.

Tips

- "Dry-clean only" on a garment tag means you have no recourse but to take it to the cleaners. A tag that says "Dry-clean" may possibly be washed by hand. Some say it is best to dry-clean a garment once to set the dyes before you start hand washing it.
- Attach a small magnetic basket to the side of the washing machine for items found in pockets.
- If you do laundry for the family, refuse to wash unpaired socks. Insist that everyone pin each pair together with sturdy safety pins or those little plastic circles into which some sock pairs will slip. If they aren't paired, you won't

wash them. Now no more pairing—big annoyance saver. Another good idea is to color code socks. Buy a different color band or sock for each individual and let him or her match.

- Time your washing machine's cycle. This will help you plan your washing schedule. If your washing machine is located in the basement, utility room, or away from the main part of the house where you can't hear it finish, set a kitchen timer to remind you to move the laundry along.

- Hang clothes directly from the dryer while they are still a little bit damp so wrinkles will not set in. Use a timer to alert you to when the dryer is finished or near finished. As you know, clothes that remain crumpled in the dryer come out wrinkled.

- As already suggested, use a dirty clothes hamper divided into two or three sections. That way you sort for washing as you put clothes in the proper place in the hamper. This avoids one of the areas of clutter in housekeeping—piles of sorted clothes on the floor, waiting their turn in the wash. Separate the whites, lights, and darks or sort in some other way that makes sense to you. If you can't find a three-in-one hamper in your locality, look at the catalog resources in the back of this book for a variety of divided hampers.

IN THE TRENCHES WITH SMART HOMEMAKERS

Years ago, I bought one of those laundry baskets that has three bins. It's been the best investment I ever made. When one of the sections (lights, darks, reds) reaches the top, it's a load, no matter what day it is! The kids (6 and 10) sort their own laundry, and I toss the baby's in there too. We keep another hamper in the bathroom for whites (socks and underwear) so that I can bleach them.

- An oft overlooked issue with laundry is that people buy clothes rather than wash them. ("I'm out of underwear? Why, I think I'll buy another package!") One secret of streamlined laundry care is to own only the amount of clothes you really need and keep on top of washing them.

- Another hidden hindrance in moving laundry forward is that there is no room in the closets or drawers for the clean clothes and linens. The laundry hamper and baskets have become the solution to an overflow-storage problem. Uh-uh! Big mistake! Own only what you have room to store when nothing is in the laundry.
- Follow the advice of Don Aslett, America's number one cleaning guru, who says he doesn't want to gross us out but he wears work clothes for a week not just a day. I am trying to figure out exactly how this works, but the lesson is clear. Wear gently worn clothes again rather than putting them in a laundry hamper. Train kids carefully in this. Left on their own they find it easier to toss clothes in the hamper than to fold or hang them for future use.

IN THE TRENCHES WITH SMART HOMEMAKERS

From Patty:

We have four kids—three teenagers—so towels were our big issue. We have a tiny, humid bathroom, so hanging six wet towels in there every day was causing a mildew problem. No one's towel would be dry for their shower the next day . . . icky! In desperation I came up with a plan. To my surprise, it solved the laundry problem as well!

I cut each bath towel into four hand-towel sized pieces, and then serged the edges. I started with twelve bath towels. Ten towels were chopped, and I saved two as guest towels, so company wouldn't freak out. Now I have two guest towels and forty bath towels! For exactly two days my kids complained about drying off with their little towels. Then they noticed that their little towel was dry the next day when they went to use it again, and thus much more comfortable to dry off with. Also, we *never* run out of clean towels any longer! The big surprise was on laundry day. Rather than washing damp, smelly towels every 2–3 days, I now throw in one small load of towels once a week. I'm in 7th heaven!

- If you don't own a serger, or you don't want to chop towels, you could do one of several things. Either barter with a friend

210

who does sew to do something for her in exchange for her sewing expertise, or simply buy some tiny towels. I liked this idea so much that I decided to stock my camper with little towels. I found a huge, inexpensive bundle of white, square hand towels in the automotive department at Sam's Club. Now we have the towel problem licked both at home and on the road!

The secret to the ironing problem can be summed up in one word—*don't*!

Ironing—the Bare Bones Way

The secret to the ironing problem can be summed up in one word—*don't*! Wherever possible, buy clothes made of double knit or other wrinkle-free material and either hang them wet to dry on the hanger or get them quickly out of the dryer and hang or fold before they wrinkle.

Use fabric softener in the wash water or dryer to further encourage smooth drying. Other dewrinkle products are available in spray form and encourage wet clothes to shed wrinkles as they dry. Here in south Florida, one can hope the industrial strength humidity will naturally steam out wrinkles, and I suppose it does to some degree. Of course, you can always use a handheld steamer that dewrinkles clothes but does not leave them crisp.

Avoiding ironing is not always possible. When it must be done, more and more the custom is becoming for individuals to iron their own clothes pretty much as they need them. Train your children to do their own as soon as they are able. Sometimes one person, usually Mom, will schedule an hour or half hour of ironing to coincide with a favorite TV program to ease the boredom.

I learned two things when I was forced to iron my cute spring cottons:

- Don't try to do the job perfectly, attending to every seam in detail. Just "mash the wrinkles out" as my family used to say. (I can feel the shudders of perfectionists around the country. I hope they don't all do it at once and cause an earth tremor.)
- Printed material does not show wrinkles as much as solid material. The wrinkles somehow become hidden in the pattern—somewhat.

If you are still using the clunkers you bought years ago, buy a good quality iron and ironing board. Make sure both the board and the iron are stored where they are easily accessible, unless you are blessed with a laundry room where they can be left set up. The board must be light and open and close easily. Nothing discourages ironing like grappling with a heavy, rebellious ironing board! You will resist getting it out until you have an emergency and, worse yet, you won't want to put it back when you are finished. Prepare to succeed.

Tips

- Avoid ironing baskets. They are black holes often used as overflow for too full closets and drawers. Keep all unironed items folded or hung where they would be placed if they were ironed. Discard old items if you don't have room to store your unironed things.
- When you sprinkle items to be ironed, do so with warm water. Roll them up and let them sit while the moisture spreads evenly throughout. If you can't iron them right away, stick them in the refrigerator but don't leave them for several days or something really funny happens to them that is hard to correct. Again, I speak from experience here.
- Hand pressing is wiping the wrinkles out with your hand. You will be surprised at how effective hand pressing can be on things like pillowcases, slips, and the like.

- Don't overload the dryer. Things will be less wrinkled if it is only about a third full.
- To prevent a fire, vacuum the lint out of your dryer exhaust once a year or so. This is one of those stitches in time that will save nine stitches of firefighting and cleanup—definitely a Bare Bones tradeoff.

Decision Time—Choose Your Top 20 Percent

Keep your choices simple. One or two significant ones are all that are necessary.

1. What physical change can you make in your setup that will improve getting your laundry done? Can you buy new equipment, move something, get rid of something?
2. What new action can you initiate to improve how laundry flows from dirty to clean, from the laundry basket to your closets and drawers? Can you train helpers, wash more often, fold and put away immediately, do something else?

Make it specific:

1. I will make this physical change:

2. I will make this action change:

14

Food Isn't Just What We Eat

Make It as Easy as Possible

We are all busy people and often do not have time to do weekly meal planning and grocery shopping. At the end of a long day we don't want to look through 150 pages of "main course" recipes to find something for the chicken in our fridge that is about to expire. Nor do we want to use the same tried and true recipe again and again. That becomes too much of a good thing.

So, try organizing your recipes in a ring notebook by meat/ main ingredient. For example, set up dividers labeled "chicken," "pork," "seafood," "ground beef," "other beef," or whatever other meats you frequently consume. Now you only have to flip through a couple of pages to find something for dinner. I often make a list of a few specific grocery items I need and then buy an assortment of fresh meats and vegetables. By organizing my recipes this way, I know I will always be able to find a quick and delicious meal within minutes.

Kasey Vejar
Simply Organized, Inc.
Shawnee Mission, Kansas
www.kcorganizers.com

Somewhere deep in the psyche, food takes on a significant psychological aura.

Food is not just fuel that keeps our bodies stoked. Somewhere deep in the psyche, food takes on a significant psychological aura.

In her article "Home for Dinner," Carla Williams tells of being moved by her teenage son, Joshua, singing "Here at the table with the family I love" from a song he had written.[1] This story spotlights how significant mealtime can be for family bonding. Williams further reports that psychologists at Syracuse University reviewed research over the last fifty years and found that families who had household routines, including eating together, had healthier children, increased marital satisfaction, and less stress. Research by the National Center on Addiction and Substance Abuse and other organizations found that children who share family dinners abuse drugs and alcohol less, have more nutritious diets, and perform better in school.

Food Isn't Just What We Cook

The family is hungry and grumpy, so we fix something. They eat, they are no longer hungry, we clean up, and it is over. Right?

Well, yes and no. The old saying about the stomach being the way to a man's heart is true not only of men

215

but of children, other family members, and friends. Eating well is one aspect of self care.

In the context of a loving family, the person who serves a delicious and satisfying meal, which the family eats together, is serving not only nutrition but caring and love. In the context of the fast-food drive-through, the employee handing the food out the window is dispensing nothing but calories and flavor, mostly in the form of sugar, salt, and fat. Though the kids may love the fare at their favorite place, these meals lack the personal touch. They go to the stomach but probably fall short of reaching the heart.

Don't get me wrong. Food is not love. We cannot substitute food for love or draw comfort from it without getting in real trouble both psychologically and physically. Nor does every meal need to be homemade and eaten together at the dining table. According to the *Journal of the American Dietetic Association*, in America 50 percent of meals are eaten outside the home. Fourteen percent of adolescents say they never eat with their families. Sixty-five percent of adolescents eat meals with their families three to seven times a week. It is easy to see from these statistics and our own experiences that the pull of modern life is away from the family dining table.

The Love Connection

We show love in many ways. Providing a supportive, clean, and orderly home is one way. Making money to meet family needs for clothing is another. So is giving time to help with projects and attend games and plays. And there are hundreds of other ways. But perhaps nothing touches the heart so much as sitting down together to a meal that Mom has provided for the family. Wonderful meals lure the family home for dinner and, later in life, for holidays. In today's busy world, we need strong attractions to draw the family together, because after a while, grabbing a bite and eating alone in front of the TV can become a habit.

Danielle Lee, thirteen, of Manchester, Michigan, expresses her desires poignantly:

> Some families have a nice family dinner, like spaghetti and meatballs and apple pie or something else yummy that the mom cooks in her free time. But both of my parents have to work. Some of my friends' moms will make dinner, and the dads will come home, and the whole family will sit and talk and have one of those really good meals. I wish we were like that. Then my busy family would have some time to talk to each other.[7]

A meal's influence starts when family members enter the house and smell the dinner cooking. Perhaps it is late in the day and the aroma of meat loaf or roast chicken wafts through the air as they enter. Or perhaps it is in the afternoon when kids come home from school and smell freshly baked cookies. Or it may be the delicious aroma of freshly baked bread (not unknown in this day of bread-making machines). Are we dreaming or what!

The story is complicated in single-parent households where one parent, usually Mom, carries the burden of day-to-day living, which often includes a full-time job. Not every "mom" is female. Over two million men are single parents. The number of single-dad households has increased 62 percent since 1992. That's one in every six single-parent families.

Home cooking is wonderful, but not everyone has the time, talent, or interest to make home-cooked meals for the family. In the long run, the family togetherness at the table is more important than how the food got there. Fortunately, although home cooking is special in many

217

ways, in today's world, there are many good alternatives to cooking from scratch.

The Bare Bones Way

Even when love is strong, the ideal of home cooking is not always possible. Your schedule, the schedules of others, or your own lack of interest or ability to cook may interfere. How can you get the best meals with the least amount of effort? As in all areas of organizing, planning the work and working a good plan are key.

Easy Meal Preparation Ideas

Plan ahead for the week's meals, noting especially what will be appropriate for your busiest days. Avoid either last-minute trips to the store or repetitious quickie preparations, like frozen fish sticks or chicken nuggets, pizza ordered in, drive-through pickups, or whatever your overused standby choice is.

Once you have the menu for the week, think each morning or the night before about your plan for dinner the next evening. This will dictate what steps you will take to get the food on the table easily. You may need to get something out of the freezer or start the Crock-Pot.

Here are some ideas that will help ease your food preparation efforts and shorten the time you have to spend:

TIME AND ENERGY SAVERS

- Have members of your family do simple preparation as soon as their age permits. With training, most children can start the oven and put in a frozen casserole by the age of ten or so. By early teens, many children can prepare and serve a whole meal. Of course, husbands may take part and even enjoy it.

- Cook together on weekends. Make it an interactive family time of togetherness.
- Some people cook once a month, freeze the dishes, and simply build the daily meals from the supply. Just be sure to use the frozen meals before they develop freezer burn or are forgotten. It is a good idea to make a list of dishes with dates and post it on the side of the refrigerator to remind you what is stored in the freezer.

EASY FOOD SOURCES

- Use frozen prepared dishes as part of the meal—the entrée, side dish, or dessert. They are getting more tasty all the time.
- Make double the amount your family will eat and freeze half for later use.
- Buy food by the pound from the deli or one of those by-the-pound stores that are so popular around the country.
- Crock-Pots or slow cookers are an easy way to prepare a meal and seem to be regaining popularity.
- Use a George Foreman grill for quick grilling of meats.
- Use Hamburger Helper® and other boxed or frozen preparations that speed up preparing a home-cooked meal. They may be your best friends and the dishes may become family classics.

Suggested Seven-Day Menu Plan

It takes some creativity to plan interesting and easy meals for a week. The following ideas will get you started, but you will want to adapt them to fit your family's tastes and your time and energy.

Sunday/Family: Large dish—meat or casserole. Make enough for two days and use the rest on Monday.

Monday/Leftover: Use the meat from Sunday's dinner for the main dish, stretching it with rice, potatoes, or gravy, or use it in a casserole. Or reheat the main dish as it is. Add deli slaw, salad, vegetable, and bread.

Tuesday: Make a vegetarian or egg dish.

Wednesday/Budget: Make a pasta dish or serve hot dogs and beans, tuna casserole, or some other low-cost dish.

Thursday/Fun food for kids or yourself: Hot dogs, hamburgers, pizza, tacos, and the like.

Friday/Quickie or express: Use a boxed helper, such as Hamburger Helper® or Tuna Helper®, or build a meal around a frozen prepared dish.

Saturday/Catch up, entertain, or eat out: Use up the leftovers. In the summer, barbecue.[3]

IN THE TRENCHES WITH SMART HOMEMAKERS

From Gwena:

I recently started a Meal Planning "system" for our family (actually 2). In one I created an actual binder with a month's menus (my dh [dear husband] gets paid bi-weekly) and we rotate between our most common and well liked meals. The other system I just started since we started homeschooling last week—a friend of mine passes down to me her mom's used *Taste of Home* and *Quick Cooking* magazines. I pull desserts and delectable meals that are quick & easy (with homeschooling 2 young, active boys I don't have much time for meal planning) to fix. I find if I have my meals planned ahead of time, I am *much* more likely to actually *cook* a meal (LOL [laugh out loud], my biggest struggle, besides disciplining our children). I try to choose several recipes for which I already have all or most of the ingredients on hand. One dessert that was delicious and my whole family loved was so simple & quick—Cool Whip, vanilla pudding mix, milk, and broken Oreo-type cookies, and chill it. Yum!! (You put it in separate dessert glasses, and then I stuck an Oreo on top like the gourmet restaurants, tee hee.)

Time-Saver Shopping List

Keep a grocery list on a whiteboard on the refrigerator and require the person who uses the last of an item to write it on the board. Copy them before you head to the store.

It's a good idea to type a master shopping list for groceries and sundries that you purchase on a regular basis. If you generally use one store, list the items in the same order as the route you follow in the store. This will help you avoid skipping things and having to backtrack. If you use specific brands and sizes, include them as part of the master list. Leave blank spaces in each section for "write in" items—seasonal products, entertainment items, and so on. After you make up the list, make photocopies of it; then post a copy in the kitchen every week. Then you and your family can simply check off the items that are needed. By being specific about brands and sizes, you make it possible for someone else to shop for you without the annoyance of "I hate this kind of ketchup!"

Clean Up as You Cook

Cooking is creative and can even be fun, but the aftermath—the cleanup—can be a drag. As you cook, develop a system of cleaning the utensils and pots as soon as

221

As you cook, develop a system of cleaning the utensils and pots as soon as you finish with them.

you finish with them. I once went to the home of a friend in rural Indiana for Sunday dinner. When I entered her house through the kitchen, I thought she had forgotten I was coming because all of the cooking things were washed, dried, and put away. The kitchen was spotless. The food was being kept hot in serving dishes. To this day, I haven't figured out how she did such a thorough job. I assume she washed, dried, and put away all cooking utensils as she put food in the serving dishes, similar to the plan described in the Trenches idea below.

But then there is the cleanup of the dishes after the meal. Some people zip dishes and other utensils quickly into the dishwasher. Others let them pile up. Use paper plates as much as possible, except of course when you are inviting special people over for Sunday dinner.

And certainly, put a spoon rest next to pots you are stirring to keep goop from getting on the stove top. Why make a mess if you can avoid it?

IN THE TRENCHES WITH SMART HOMEMAKERS

Pot Pileup:
The newest habit that I have been able to incorporate has been to wash the pots and pans as soon as I empty them. I used to empty the food from them, and then let them sit on the stove. The food would dry to a hard crust, which would take ten times as long to clean whenever I got around to it. If I can't wash them out right away, I immediately fill them with soapy water to prevent the food from caking on. Then I try to get to it before the night is over (I rarely wait until the next day—seems that when the water gets cold and the grease floats to the top, I am less motivated to wash the pot than when it's full of hot,

sudsy water). This one simple habit has been a lifesaver for me—the rewards are so great that I feel it is less pain to clean them *now*, while it's easy, than the pain of waiting until *later* and discovering that the pot I needed to use right at that moment is dirty. My once infamous "pots & pans pileup" is now a thing of my past.

Little habits can make the biggest differences!

Decision Time—Choose Your Top 20 Percent

Write *yes* or *no* beside each statement. Celebrate your *yes* answers. Consider how to improve the *no* answers.

____ I value consistently gathering for a daily meal as a family.

____ I prepare good meals as a regular thing.

____ I plan a menu for each week.

____ I start meals ahead when necessary.

____ I ask for the assistance of others in the family.

____ I know and use commercially prepared food to supplement my own cooking.

____ I have favorite recipes available for use.

____ I have an efficient system for shopping for groceries.

Look at your *no* answers. Which one or ones do you want to think of changing? How would you make the change? Remember, think of a little change that will make a big difference. You may wish to address several ideas covered in this chapter. Then finish the following sentence.

In an effort to make cooking and all that goes with it less of a burden, I will:

15
■

You and Your Car Take Care of Each Other

Reminders about Car Organizing

- To have all the things you need for your day, use a task basket that leaves with you in the morning and comes in with you at the end of the day. While at home, drop things into the basket that will be needed for errands, such as store returns or things to deliver. While out, drop things in the basket that need to come in at the end of the day.
- To avoid messie-distractions, use plastic containers that can snug between seats or can rest safely on the floor to hold drinks. If a spill happens, the bucket catches it,

not your upholstery or carpet. Also, cover the seats with washable towels if you have a messy crew or lifestyle.

- To stay safe, purchase the roadside assistance option your insurance company offers as an add-on to your policy. It's inexpensive peace of mind. Keep important phone numbers posted on your visor in case of emergency, including your own cell phone number, your insurance agent's number, and the special roadside assistance number. If you have to call for assistance, be ready to give good cross-street references to your location. Ask the name of the service that will be coming to you. Be cautious. When help is dispatched, your location will be announced over public airwaves and anyone could come to your location before the true help you actually called for arrives.

Linda Durham
Organizing Matters
Houston Texas
www.organizingmatters.com

Messy cars show up in the strangest places. In *The Wailing Wind*, a mystery by Tony Hillerman, the detective searched a suspect's car, he

began extracting odds and ends from Mrs. McKay's floorboards—starting with a Baby Ruth wrapper, a crumpled tissue, a paper cup, a wrapper from a McDonald's hamburger, and a cigarette butt. . . . By the time he had completed his search of both sides of the front seat and moved to the back, his box was almost half filled with wildly assorted trash, evidence that Mrs. McKay was a regular customer of various fast-food establishments and a person who saved Wal-Mart advertising sections, discount coupons, empty cigarette packages, and even the high heel from a black slipper.[1]

If any part of this picture looks familiar, read on.

The Rolling Room

The car holds a unique place in organizing because it is one place where you can't close the door or pull the curtain to hide its condition. Au contraire, you take it out of the garage or yard and parade it all over town. Anybody can walk by and look right inside.

> The car holds a unique place in organizing because it is one place where you can't close the door or pull the curtain to hide its condition.

Since this is a book on organizing, the emphasis is going to be on maintaining the inside seating area and the outside finish of the car. Of course, the mechanical parts need to be tended to regularly, usually by taking it to a mechanic for servicing. The other parts are hands-on responsibility and more within our control.

Out of curiosity, I have surveyed the condition of cars by walking around parking lots and peering inside some of them. Sometimes I have to work hard to see through the tinted windows. Eventually, I may be arrested for my skulking activity. I have been surprised—nay, amazed—at how neat many cars are inside. It makes me realize that when my car is messy, I am way out of step with the norm. Keeping the car neat is important because my neatness and your neatness, or lack thereof, is evident to the world. For most of us, looking neat in front of our friends is important.

The car is frequently used as an extension of the house, an additional rolling room—or rooms. For some, it is an office where papers are tossed, a dining room in which to eat, a bedroom for napping, a family room for visiting and listening to music, and a storage room for overflow belongings.

Of course, the car is transportation as well, taking us to school, shopping, work, conferences, concerts, and the beach, which means crumbs, pillows, tapes, CDs, ticket stubs, class notes, business papers, seashells, and the like may all be found there.

In addition, the car acts as a truck when it carries school supplies, purchases, maybe plants, building supplies, and whatever needs to be transported into—and hopefully away from—the house. All of that transporting may leave behind bags, boxes, receipts, dirt, and things your arms are too full to carry.

Vans are even harder to maintain. Videos, mildewed bathing suits from a trip to the beach, physical education clothes from the last day of school, and a multitude of other leftovers can gather undetected in the back for months.

Put that way, it sounds like it takes a lot of work to maintain the car. Not so! There are a few basic rules of the Bare Bones Way, which, if consistently applied, will leave you with a car you will be proud to parade around town.

Because it is a small area, the car is the ideal spot for practicing organizational skills and habits.

What Do You Want?

Why do you want to take good care of your car? Below, check each reason that is important to you. Put two checks if something is especially important.

____ its resale value

____ to feel good each time I get in it

____ to feel good when I give others a ride

____ to impress neighbors, coworkers, and valet

____ it is the right thing to do

____ so it will last longer

The Bare Bones of Car Care

The paint on my six-year-old car began to disappear in spots about as big as a freckle. After enough freckles appeared, the undercoat showed through noticeably. The salesman had told us that new cars did not need waxing because they had a special finish. He said waxing would remove the special finish. When does the special finish lose its effectiveness? Obviously in our case somewhere before six years.

When we bought a newer used car, I set out in search of how to avoid the freckled look. I asked lots of friends and branched out into casual acquaintances with my questioning. My research into the question leads me to believe that the problem of how to care for a car finish is beyond the knowledge of the ordinary citizen. There are several possible approaches. They range from those who never wash or wax ("a car is just transportation to me") to those who make car waxing and detailing a hobby. Here are some observations from my random survey:

My friend Alan is a neat guy in many, possibly all, areas of this life. This is particularly true when it comes to his cars. He has a few easy-to-follow rules in addition to some rules only Alan and a few other enthusiasts will want to follow. Every day there is dew (which is 90 percent of the time in south Florida where he lives), Alan uses a chamois on his car in the morning. He never waxes and has never been through a car wash in his life. He claims the daily chamois will clean and brighten any finish. Just between us, I think I see some freckles appearing.

Benson, owner of a service station, hired college students to wax and machine buff his car every week. Eventually they buffed off all the paint, revealing the undercoat, but the undercoat really shone.

Bob does nothing to his car. The sides look like new but paint is peeling from the hood and top like a very, very bad case of sunburn. The sun's rays shine at a more direct angle on the top of the car, so it deteriorates faster.

John waxes his car every week, alternating two different kinds of waxes for maximum benefit. He is a car waxing enthusiast.

As students, my husband and I lived in a garage apartment behind a mansion in Columbia, South Carolina. Our landlady had one hobby, which she described as "chasing dirt." Part of her cleaning hobby was to Simonize (trust me, this is a very hard wax to apply) one part of her car every Saturday morning—right fender one week, left fender the next, hood the next. And on she went, circling around the car one part at a time. I don't recall how effective it was but the concept is certainly intriguing.

Aside from personal preferences, part of the reason there is not just one right way to care for a car finish is because car needs vary from one area of the country to the other. Country dust and dirt are different from city grime and industrial pollution. A car exposed to snow, slush, and salt has different needs from a car in the Sun Belt, which requires wax to protect it from the ultraviolet rays of the sun, in the same way its owner needs SPF lotion on his or her skin.

With our new car, I wanted to avoid the problem we had had with the other car, but I did not want to do excessive work to maintain the finish. In other words,

I was looking for the Bare Bones Way to get the job done. I had just about decided I would have to contact car manufacturers for advice when I stumbled across the owner's guide in the glove compartment of the car. And there on page 194 was a picture of a foamy bucket of water and a sponge on the page with the heading, "Washing and Waxing Your Car." This was the official word, and it was just what I needed.

Simply put, it said this:

- Wash your car with a quality car wash detergent, not strong detergent or soap.
- Wax your car with carnauba or synthetic-based wax when water stops beading up on the surface, about every three or four months.
- If you take your car through a commercial car wash (preferably one without brushes) and have wax applied, clean the wiper blades and windshield afterward to remove the wax.

There you go! Three sentences sums it up. Can't get more Bare Bones than that! It is sure a lot better than the daily chamois or the weekly waxing, which I would never do anyway.

There is one more thing, but I didn't want to make four sentences so I left it out. Here it is: Clean off gasoline spills, tree sap, insect remains, road salt, industrial fallout, and bird poop as soon as possible, or it may harm the finish.

I think my personal Bare Bones method is going to be to wax the car once a year by hand or maybe do the piecemeal thing or have it done professionally, and go through the car wash and wax cycle every three or four months, taking care to clean the wax off the windshield and wiper blades.

IN THE TRENCHES WITH SMART HOMEMAKERS

From Renee:

I am *so* glad I cleaned out the car the other day. Today the director of the day care was having car problems and asked me for a ride home. There were only a couple things that I needed to toss in the backseat so that she could sit down.

Bare Bones Car General Info

Don't let your car become a garbage can. Keep a litterbag in the car, encourage family members to use it, and empty it every time you stop where there is a trash receptacle or when you go in the house. If you have kids, encourage them to FEED MR. TRASH CAN. Put a note up for them (or yourself) in the car until removing all trash from the car and putting it in the trash can is a habit. Including a picture on the note of a hungry trash can being fed might help a lot. Put more zip in your FEED MR. TRASH CAN project for children by offering a reward, such as a nickel to the first child to spot a trash can. He or she can do the "feeding."

Don't let your car become your junk room. Each time you leave the car, check to see if there's something in it that needs to be brought into the house. Then make sure you put it where it belongs immediately once you get into the house.

Don't use the glove compartment as a junk box. Save it for maps, the car operator's manual, and a flashlight. Remember, if you get rid of the junk on a regular basis, you won't need anyplace to put it!

Stash an extra key in your wallet or purse, just in case you lose your keys or lock them in the car (something that never happens to you, right?). To be doubly sure, keep an extra car key in a small magnetic box somewhere under the car exterior. Remember where

231

Each time you leave the car, check to see if there's something in it that needs to be brought into the house.

you put it and don't announce it to the whole world—it's only for your use, not for someone who needs a car in a hurry.

Fill your car completely each time you need gas. It saves time and effort.

Beyond Bare Bones Info

Be sure you have any necessary tools—shovels, emergency flares, chains, jumper cables, and whatever fits your location and lifestyle—in the trunk of your car. Wrap them in a pad or blanket to keep them from rattling around. Also be sure to have a first aid kit in the trunk. If you live in a climate where weather can be deadly in winter, keep blankets and some canned food in the trunk. Keep it there summer and winter if you think you will forget to put it there when the weather turns cold.

For emergencies, stash an old piece of heavy plastic or worn-out plastic rain slicker in the trunk to kneel on if you have to change a tire (or for the kind soul who stops to help). Keep an extra quart of oil in an old liquid detergent bottle in the trunk. When you need it, you won't have to grapple with can openers and you can easily keep what you don't use.

In a shoe box or a box of similar size, store small essentials—paper towels, wet wipes, pen, pad of paper, extra comb—under the front seat. Don't use it as a junk box.

Place a reminder to wax the car every three or four months on your yearlong calendar or in your electronic reminder, just in case you don't notice the water is not beading up on the finish anymore.

Tips

- Use net bath scrubbers to remove bird poop and bugs from the car surface. They are soft and won't scratch the surface.
- Rubber bands around each end of the car's sun visors will hold maps, directions, and other items you want to keep close at hand but out of the car seat.
- Use a commercial car wash rather than do it by hand.
- If washing by hand, wash from the top and work your way down. Don't wash a car in the sun or while the engine is hot because it makes the hood hot and that makes streaks.
- Blow dirt out of the car by using a leaf blower. It works faster than vacuuming.
- Clean salt from under the car by putting a lawn sprinkler under the car and turning it on full blast.
- Wax a reluctant car antenna or rub it with waxed paper.
- Line the trunk with a rug remnant if you carry messy things often.
- The car has a practical use not often considered. Women like to put on makeup in the car, not because they are running late necessarily but because the daylight is better than the light in the house. This is a good idea but please not while you're driving!

Decision Time—Choose Your Top 20 Percent

What will make the greatest impact on the condition of your car with the least effort? Write below your new habit or schedule for the inside and the outside of your car.

I will do this to the inside of the car:

I will do this to the outside of the car:

Part 3

Living the Plan

16

Live Your Best Life

Because a house is so much more than a place to live, we describe it with the more personal word *home*. Home is where we meet ourselves and remind ourselves who we are and what is important to us. It tells an ever-changing story of who we are. It protects what is significant to us, our comfort, our values, and what we love. Because it reflects a sense of self, home begins within us. Because we are significant, our home is significant as well.

The creation of home that flows from who you are slowly transforms your surroundings to match who you are inside. When the structure, function, and appearance reflect accurately and gracefully who you (and your family) are, you have created a home.

Sometimes women tell me they spend a lot of time away from home because it is so messy and they don't want to face it. Since, for a woman, the house is her larger self, this is a significant alienation from herself. But when things are going right, the heart soars.

IN THE TRENCHES WITH SMART HOMEMAKERS

Aleen to Marjorie:

Marjorie, I used to think the way you do. It was always my "house." I found that when I started thinking of it as my "home," my motivation went up. I got more done. I actually found myself "wanting" to clean. I also find that I am prouder of my accomplishments in the decluttering process. Now, I still often fall into the "house" terminology. Habit, familiarity of feeling, etc. causing that. So I try to keep reminding myself, this is my "home." When I scan the cleaned areas, I think "home." Like Dorothy in the Wizard of Oz. "There's no place like *home*."

I think that the term "house" is like "apartment." It implies a sense of impermanence and ownership without pride. Sort of like "my pencil," "my shoes," etc. So maybe if we all start thinking of our residence as a "home" rather than a "house" or "apartment" or "condo" or "trailer," the decluttering process might become easier.

Have you ever noticed how people often name their vehicles but seldom their homes?

Love Affair with the House

Whether we like it or not, we have a love affair going with our houses. As in all intimate relationships, it is reciprocal. We shape our house as it shapes us. We lavish time, money, attention, and creativity on its development. In return, it supports and succors us. Our house provides sanctuary, pleasure, and comfort. It offers a space both for private renewal and socializing with family and friends. Our house is easy to lose this larger perspective amid the household tips, mundane chores, and just plain business.

Life Is Simple

Life is simple. But living it can become complex. Struggling to see through the complexity to the simple (to the Bare Bones, if you will), people have tried to state in a few words what is really important in life.

- When Polonius gave Hamlet "the talk" about life, he told him to be true to himself and then he could not be false to any man. Kipling wrote a whole poem for his son focusing on how to "be a man, my son."
- Anna Quindlen, in her book *A Short Guide to a Happy Life*, says:

  I suppose the best piece of advice I could give anyone is very simple: Get a life. A real life, not a manic pursuit of the next promotion, the biggest paycheck, the larger house. Do you think you'd care so much about those things if you developed an aneurysm one afternoon, or found a lump in your breast while in the shower?[1]

  Looking at one's mortality clarifies better than anything what is truly important.

- Children who study the Shorter Catechism are taught that the "chief end of man" is to "glorify God and to enjoy Him forever." The prophet Micah narrows his observation down to one stirring sentence, "What does the LORD require of you? To act justly and to love mercy and to walk humbly with your God" (Micah 6:8). Most important, of course, are the words of Jesus, who told us that a love relationship with God and loving others are of supreme importance (see Matt. 22:37–39).

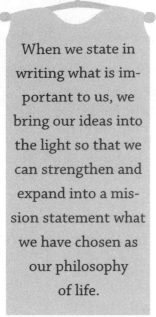

When we state in writing what is important to us, we bring our ideas into the light so that we can strengthen and expand into a mission statement what we have chosen as our philosophy of life.

Which of these teachings do you most deeply buy into? Or is it another teaching? How do you view your prime directive and how are you going to live in the light of that directive? What are you going to build into it? Because you can't do everything, you will find you need to prune out things that have crept in that do not support your real priorities.

Every person has a principle or a few principles of some kind that govern his or her life. When we state in writing what is important to us, we bring our ideas into the light so that we can strengthen and expand into a mission statement what we have chosen as our philosophy of life.

Expanding Your Vision

Let us suppose that a person of faith decides that his or her mission statement is to love and serve God, to love others, and to care for himself or herself in a responsible way. Stating his or her priorities in one sentence points the person in the direction he or she wants to go. However, one sentence is not enough to clarify how this is going to be played out in life. In the chapter on time management, we looked at how to make practical decisions in keeping with our top five priorities. These are pragmatic applications of our mission statement and may vary with different stages of life.

Here, however, let's take a longer-range view. We may call it our lifetime vision. It is an expansion of our mission statement. A wise proverb tells us that where there is no vision, the people perish.

Perhaps the easiest way to expand your mission statement into a lifetime vision is to fast-forward and pretend you are hearing your own eulogies at your funeral from various people who are important to you in your life. No, we are not getting morbid here; it is just that this is a good way to develop a broad view of your life. Assuming you lived by your prime directive, how did you play it out, using your particular talents in your particular circumstances? As you think, or preferably write, your lifetime vision, be specific in what people in these different areas say about you. Remember, these eulogies will tell only of the things you did right, because you envision you lived out your prime directive well.

Answer the questions that apply to you:

- What do you want your children to say about you?
- Your grandchildren?
- Your spouse?
- Those you worked with, including your boss?
- Your church?
- Your friends?
- The poor and needy?
- (Tongue in cheek) what would your house say about you?
- What would you say about yourself in this imaginary scene?
- Most important of all, what would God say about how you lived out your prime directive?

It is not too late to make these eulogies you desire come true, not so we can brag about ourselves but so that we can live our lives to fulfill to the max the purpose for which we were put on the earth.

Veering toward Chaos

Of course, as we go about our daily activities, there will be flotsam and jetsam that call for our attention. The car breaks down. The phone service needs to be changed. A child breaks a finger. The chicken for dinner goes bad. Someone steals our identity. Everyday concerns can suck vitality from the transcendent meaning of life if we let them.

Sometimes overwhelming tragedies dwarf our best-laid plans. A hurricane, tornado, or flood sweeps into our lives. Serious illness knocks at the door or enters our lives to stay. We lose a loved one. Unspeakable loss buckles our spirit.

The well-established law of thermodynamics is always at work: Things consistently veer toward disorder and disintegration. Your job, should you choose to accept it, is to fold each one of those complexities into the overall goal and continue to refocus your life on what is important.

And how can you do that? Your spirit needs to be ready, of course. That is a given. But so do your house, your habits, and your general patterns of living. We cannot handle well the important opportunities and demands of life from a place of organizational weakness. Now is the time to get things in order and to establish patterns to your life, to build a simple grid on which the complexities can be handled.

IN THE TRENCHES WITH SMART HOMEMAKERS

From Jennifer:

Since I've been having some successes lately, I thought I'd share. I'm tickled pink with the improvements!

The neatest thing has been to be able to maintain a clean area once I spent a few hours on it. The kitchen is clean, dishes are washed shortly after meals, laundry is washed in a timely fashion, the stairway to the 2nd floor is cleared of "stuff," the sofa can be used for sitting (not piles), horizontal areas are free to gather dust (not piles) if I choose to let them (!!) and etc. Maintaining takes only a *fraction* of the time compared with decluttering and deep-cleaning (not the dirt kind, the "stuff" kind).

This is wonderful motivation for me. It is so freeing that I have no desire to gloat about it or show it off; I am just enjoying the freedom immensely!

Fighting the Right Fight

On the news I was listening to an official of a country that has been at war for many years. The cost of war has taken a heavy toll on the citizens' quality of life. Chronic problems continue and needs go unmet because maintaining security requires so much time and energy. Dealing with security has drained away the quality of life in that country. Education, the arts, social services, and libraries have all been neglected.

Struggling with organization will do the same to our personal lives. A life that is organized frees you up to pursue what is really important to you and to your family. Freeing yourself from the 80 percent that produces little of importance in your life will save tons of time and energy that you can then put into improving the quality of your life. Concentrating on the significant 20 percent that pays off sets your life up organizationally to do what really matters in other areas.

Look at your prime directives, the priorities that focus your life. Make them into statements. In the light of these directives, what would you do differently if you weren't so busy and stressed? Maybe you don't have the slightest idea because you have been so busy keeping up day-to-day living that you've never thought about what your priorities should be. This life is not a dress rehearsal.

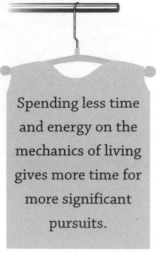

Spending less time and energy on the mechanics of living gives more time for more significant pursuits.

We don't get another chance. It's super-important we live this life thoughtfully and well. Don't let the daily struggles squeeze out your ability to identify and pursue goals that give true meaning to your existence.

Bare Bones Organizing for Abundant Living

Spending less time and energy on the mechanics of living gives more time for more significant pursuits. That's what the Bare Bones Way is all about.

In keeping with her approach to life, Della applied the Bare Bones approach to the ideas she found in the Bible. She divided her life into three areas: God, others, and self.

First, she clearly defined how her commitment to God would play out in her life. At home she would spend time each day in Bible reading and prayer. She would also dedicate her home to showing hospitality as a part of reaching out to comfort and help others. She was going to attend worship services regularly at her church, become a contributing member of a small group study there, and volunteer to help with the women's ministry. Although there was ample occasion to do much more, she felt good that she had defined her commitments and boundaries so she did not feel guilty if she refused an additional task. She knew how and why to say no.

When she thought of others, she focused on her family first and then friends. Della decided she needed to make up a three-week menu and rotate it. That way she would know the groceries to buy and the meals to prepare so that her family would be well fed.

She set up and implemented a simple schedule for the family, so the kids learned how to manage their lives and so the house was always in good condition for family time.

She had read John Wesley's straightforward advice:

> Do all the good you can,
> By all the means you can,
> In all the ways you can,
> In all the places you can,
> At all the times you can,
> To all the people you can,
> As long as ever you can.

Though in her heart she desired to serve others, she considered the limits of her time and energy. As a result, she decided she would serve thoughtfully, balancing it with other obligations. In other words, she would set priorities in this regard and then maintain boundaries around them.

When she turned her attention to herself—a very important part of her balanced life—she felt she should streamline her wardrobe to have only a few basics that mixed and matched. She modernized her makeup, keeping it simple, and asked her hairstylist for an easy-care (but attractive) cut. She decided to leave work on time and not bring work home. She found to her surprise that by making simple adjustments in how she functioned at work, it was possible to keep this commitment. Finally, she decided to walk in an air-conditioned mall in her neighborhood three days a week.

In short, she sharpened her focus on things that were important in her life and sought simple ways of implementing them. A lot of unimportant extras fell by the wayside. She had time to add a hobby she dearly loved—oil painting. She realized what an important part

243

it had played in her life and how much she had missed it. The change in how her life worked was palpable. She spent less time working on the stuff of life and spent more time living it.

A small part of our time needs to be spent organizing the stage for the play we call our lives. How well you do this will determine whether you will become a woman of good intentions or a woman of influence. This book urges you to organize simply yet specifically. Then live out your life abundantly. Live it out joyfully. Don't just leave behind general memories; leave behind a heritage. Free yourself from complexity, so you can live your life significantly. Make it truly sing.

Decision Time

What is your prime directive or mission statement? Make it one sentence if possible.

What is your vision for your life, based on insights you had when thinking about your eulogies?

Are there any activities that need to be pruned from your life because they don't fit your prime directive and your vision? What are they?

17

A Quick Review—
Your Plan for Progress

The Heart of the Book

The heart of this book consists of ten powerful ideas that will transform your house and life. The first three ideas get the house under control; the last seven keep it that way. You are encouraged to latch onto the ten concepts for order and do whatever it takes to incorporate them into your life.

3 Steps *to Organize the House*

1. Consolidate—Group everything together with like items.
2. Containerize—Store them in an appropriate place in containers with labels.

245

3. Condense—Get rid of duplicates and unused, un-wanted, or unneeded items.

2 Routines *That Maintain the House*

1. Do four things in the morning.
2. Do four things at night.

5 Habits *to Keep Clutter on the Run*

1. If you get it out, put it away.
2. Apply the thirty-second rule consistently—if it takes thirty seconds or less to do something, do it immediately.
3. Follow the camping rule—leave a room the way you found it.
4. Look, really look at your surroundings.
5. Use little minutes to clean.

Decision Time—What Will You Do First?

There are many organizing suggestions in this book. Ignore 80 percent of them for now. Choose to implement only those few that will impact your life as it is now.

Of the topics we have covered, where are your hot spots, the ones that, if changed, would make a significant impact in your life? Choose a few, perhaps five, maybe fewer, from the Decision Time sections at the end of each chapter. Write them down and post them with a time plan so you will remember to work on them consistently.

There are other improvements that you may choose to make later. But in true Bare Bones fashion, focus on the most important now and let the others take care of themselves.

Notes

Chapter 1 Improving Your Quality of Life

1. Miriam Lukken, *Mrs. Dunwoody's Excellent Instructions for Homekeeping* (New York: Warner, 2003), xii.
2. Ibid.
3. Ibid., xiii.

Chapter 2 Get a Simple Plan and Simply Work the Plan

1. *Miami Herald*, Feb. 23, 2003.

Chapter 3 Organizing the House the Bare Bones Way

1. Mel Levine, *The Myth of Laziness* (New York: Simon and Schuster, 2003), 138.

Chapter 4 Managing Your Time and Life

1. Alan Lakein, *How to Get Control of Your Time and Your Life* (New York: New American Library, 1973).

Chapter 7 Living Rooms, Bathrooms, and Beyond

1. *Parade* (Sept. 21, 2003).
2. *Tween Ages* magazine, published by Focus on the Family (Sept. 2003), quoting statistics first appearing in the *Washington Post*.

Chapter 8 You Can Clean Your House in Fifteen Minutes a Day—or Maybe Thirty on a Bad Day

1. Don Aslett, *Do I Dust or Vacuum First?* (Cincinnati: Writer's Digest Books, 1982).
2. Cheryl Mendelson, *Home Comforts: The Art and Science of Keeping House* (New York: Scribner, 1999).
3. Don Aslett, *Is There Life after Housework?* (Cincinnati: Writer's Digest Books, 1992).

Chapter 9 The Fam—Friend or Foe

1. James Dobson, *Focus on the Family* radio program, May 2, 2003.
2. Sandra Felton, *Neat Moms, Messie Kids* (Grand Rapids: Revell, 2002).

Chapter 14 Food Isn't Just What We Eat

1. Carla Williams, "Home for Dinner," *Focus on Your Child* (July/August 2003): 1.
2. *Parade* (Sept. 21, 2003).
3. This is adapted from the ideas found on www.7daymenuplanner.com.

Chapter 15 You and Your Car Take Care of Each Other

1. Tony Hillerman, *The Wailing Wind* (New York: Harper, 2002), 276.

Chapter 16 Live Your Best Life

1. Anna Quindlen, *A Short Guide to a Happy Life* (New York: Random House, 2000).

Resources

Books

Books on organizing life fall into several categories. To complement the topics of this book, you may want to look into some of the topics and books below.

If I wanted more information on improving my life organizationally, I would go to my local bookstore and look for books in the household section. The latest books on organizing including some classics are nestled among the books on decorating and home repair. Books about taking control of and simplifying one's life are scattered throughout the self-improvement section.

A second place I would look, depending on its proximity, is the local library. It may or may not have the latest books, but it will have books that are no longer on the bookstore shelves. The oldies are often the goodies.

The third place to look is at an online bookstore. Type in the words *household organizing* (if you put in *organizing* alone, you may get information on starting a union) or *simplicity*. Look to see if reviews of books by other readers are available.

I encourage you to refer to my other books, all published by Revell: *The New Messies Manual*—the flagship book for change; *The Messie Motivator*; *Messie No More*; *Neat Mom, Messie Kids*; and *When You Live with a Messie*.

Simplicity

Davidson, Jeff. *Breathing Space: Living and Working at a Comfortable Pace in a Sped-up Society*. New York: MasterMedia Limited, 1991.

Jones, Sheila, ed. *Finding Balance*. Billerica, MA: Discipleship Publications, 2002.

Time Management

Davidson, Jeff. *The Complete Idiot's Guide to Managing Your Time*. New York: Alpha Books, 1995.

Macgee-Cooper, Ann, with Duane Trammell. *Time Management for Unmanageable People*. New York: Bantam, 1994.

Otto, Donna. *Get More Done in Less Time*. Eugene, OR: Harvest House, 1995.

Clutter

Aslett, Don. *Not for Packrats Only: How to Clean Up, Clear Out, and Dejunk Your Life Forever*. New York: Penguin, 1991.

Campbell, Jeff. *Clutter Control: Putting Your Home on a Diet*. New York: Dell, 1992.

Neziroglu, Fugen, Jerome Bubrick, and Tobias Yaryura. *Overcoming Compulsive Hoarding*. Oakland: New Harbinger, 2004.

Organizing

Cilley, Marla. *Sink Reflections*. New York: Bantam, 2002.

Lockwood, Georgene. *The Complete Idiot's Guide to Organizing Your Life*. New York: Alpha Books, 1996.

Mendelson, Cheryl. *Home Comforts: The Art and Science of Keeping House*. New York: Scribner, 1999.

Rich, Jason. *The Everything Organize Your Home Book: Straighten Up the Entire House, from Cleaning Your Closets to Reorganizing Your Kitchen*. Avon, MA: Adams Media, 2002.

Roth, Eileen, with Elizabeth Miles. *Organizing for Dummies*. New York: Hungry Minds, 2002.

Williams, Debbie. *Put Your House in Order: Organizing Strategies Straight from the Word*. Houston: Let's Get It Together, 2002.

Paper Organizing Tips

Barnes, Emilie. *The Fifteen-Minute Organizer*. Eugene, OR: Harvest House, 1991.

Smallin, Donna. *Unclutter Your Home: Seven Simple Steps, Seven Hundred Tips and Ideas*. Pownal, VT: Storey Books, 1999.

Winston, Stephanie. *Best Organizing Tips*. New York: Simon and Schuster, 1996.

Parenting

Elkind, David. *The Hurried Child: Growing Up Too Fast Too Soon*. Cambridge, MA: Perseus, 2001.

Felton, Sandra. *Neat Mom, Messie Kids*. Grand Rapids: Revell, 2002.

Rosenfield, Alvin, and Nicole Wise. *The Over-Scheduled Child: Avoiding the Hyper-Parenting Trap*. New York: St. Martin's, 2000.

Tinglof, Christina Baglivi. *The Organized Parent: Three Hundred Sixty-Five Simple Solutions to Managing Your Home, Your Time, and Your Family's Life.* New York: Contemporary Books, 2002.

Websites about Organizing

Websites have a limited life, but by using a search engine, you will be able to find many that can help.

www.messies.com—The website of Messies Anonymous, founded by Sandra Felton. Contains a lot of information for those who struggle with disorder in their lives. Join online groups for regular support in making changes.

http://groups.yahoo.com/group/The-Organizer-Lady— Sign up for daily encouragement and reminders from Sandra Felton to keep on track and in focus.

www.OnlineOrganizing.com—"A world of organizing solutions." Read excellent articles, join discussion groups, get questions answered by professional organizers.

www.OrganizersWebRing.com—Professional Organizers Web Ring or POWR. Their motto is "You've got the POWR to get organized." Find a professional organizer in your area and read articles on many subjects that affect your everyday organizing life.

www.nsgcd.org—National Study Group on Chronic Disorganization. "The premier online resource for anyone interested (personally or professionally) in Chronic Disorganization."

www.napo.net—National Association of Professional Organizers. Locate a professional organizer in your area or learn how to become one.

www.faithfulorganizers.com—This is a website for Christian Professional Organizers. It is the only place where faith and professional organizing meet. This site helps people all over the country locate professional organizers in their area who also share their values. They are a resource for churches to find speakers for their women's groups and moms' groups.

Catalogs for Organizing

The Container Store catalog at www.containerstore.com or 800-733-3532. They offer many organizing solutions for the home or office, including closet design, with free personalized planning service in the stores, over the phone, and online.

Get Organized catalog at www.shopgetorganized.com or 800-803-9400. Check out their many "space-saving innovations to unclutter your life."

Hold Everything catalog at www.holdeverything.com is a catalog of storage and household ideas from Williams-Sonoma.

Lillian Vernon catalogs at www.lillianvernon.com or 800-545-5426. Their household organizing catalogs *Neat Ideas* emphasize decorative organizers and tools for every room in the house.

Organize-Everything catalog at www.organize-everything .com has clothing storage items.

Organize It catalog at www.organize-it.com has lots of clothing storage products.

The Storage Store at www.thestoragestore.com has a nice variety of storage boxes.

Catalogs for Cleaning

Clean Report, from Don Aslett, America's Number One Source for Cleaning Information at www.cleanreport .com or 800-451-2402. Don has available many books and videos on cleaning as well as cleaning tools and products.

Home Improvements: Hundreds of Quick and Clever Problem-Solvers! at www.improvementscatalog.com or 800-642-2112 has lots of interesting things for use around the home, including many unique organizing products.

Home Trends at www.hometrendscatalog.com or 800-810-2340. This catalog emphasizes cleaning products but offers organizing products as well.

High- and Low-Tech Cleaning Schedule Resources

The Flipper is a system of organizing cleaning jobs available from Messies Anonymous. For information: www.messies.com or check how you can make your own in *The New Messies Manual* or *The Messies Superguide.*

The Internet has several cleaning schedule lists available online from various groups. A recent search on Google under "household cleaning schedule" turned up 5621 links, several of which looked excellent.

Create your own daily schedule using your computer calendar or online reminders, which may come with your provider service.

Online Cooking Resources

Type *recipes* in your search engine, and your poor little computer will sag with the weight of the responses.

Check out www.30daygourmet.com for cook and freeze suggestions.

Filing Resources

Hemphill, Barbara. *Taming the Paper Tiger at Home.* Washington, D.C.: Kiplinger, 2002.

Sandra Felton is the founder and president of Messies Anonymous, committed to those who seek a new and better way of life. She is the author of nearly a dozen books on bringing order and beauty to the home. Through her encouragement and unique perspective, many have been able to establish organization and harmony in their life, home, and family. Known as the Organizer Lady™, Sandra is a well-known and entertaining speaker at conferences and is a frequent guest on national radio and TV. For more information, log on to www.messies.com.

Other books by Sandra Felton

Living Organized
The Messie Motivator
Messie No More
Messies Superguide
Neat Moms, Messie Kids
The New Messies Manual
When You Live with a Messie